6/7

905

7668

LIKE A ROLLING STONE

LIKE A
ROLLING STONE
THE STRANGE LIFE OF A TRIBUTE BAND

STEVEN KURUTZ

BROADWAY BOOKS
NEW YORK

PUBLISHED BY BROADWAY BOOKS

Copyright © 2008 by Steven Kurutz

Published in the United States by Broadway Books, an imprint of The Doubleday
Broadway Publishing Group, a division of Random House, Inc., New York.
www.broadwaybooks.com

BROADWAY BOOKS and its logo, a letter B bisected on the diagonal,
are trademarks of Random House, Inc.

"Shine a Light." Written by Mick Jagger & Keith Richards © 1972. Renewed ABKCO
Music, Inc. www.abkco.com

Book design by Ruth Lee-Mui

Library of Congress Cataloging-in-Publication Data
Kurutz, Steven.
Like a Rolling Stone / by Steven Kurutz. — 1st ed.
    p.   cm.
1. Sticky Fingers (Musical group : New Jersey) 2. Tribute bands. I. Title.

ML421.S793K87 2008
782.42166092'2 — dc22   2007018334

ISBN 978-0-385-51890-1

PRINTED IN THE UNITED STATES OF AMERICA

10 9 8 7 6 5 4 3 2 1

First Edition

For Suzanne

LIKE A ROLLING STONE

1

When Glen Carroll travels for work, he takes a pair of black stage pants, a studded belt, and a few shirts, usually in splashy colors like bright red or banana yellow. If he wants to make a more noticeable impression, he might take something flashier, like a cape fashioned from an American flag and a British flag tied together, or a T-shirt imprinted with the Greek omega symbol and paired with a silk scarf, or white football pants with blue knee pads and Capezio dance shoes—an outfit very similar, as it happens, to the one Mick Jagger wore on the Rolling Stones' 1981 tour. For Glen, verisimilitude in dress is part of the job. As the singer of Sticky Fingers, which bills itself as "the leading international Rolling Stones tribute show," he is a kind of rock star proxy, a substitute Mick. And considering that the Rolling Stones tour only once every few years, and that Sticky Fingers has toured every year for the past eighteen years, it's likely that he has sung "Start Me Up," and "Brown Sugar," and "(I Can't Get No) Satisfaction" more times than Mick Jagger himself.

Glen is slim and snake-hipped, with heavy-lidded eyes and a prominent, almost coltish mouth. At forty-seven, he resembles a slightly younger Mick Jagger—the Jagger of, say, *Steel Wheels*—and wears his brown hair in the same style: short in front, longer and feathery on the sides. Offstage, he favors blue jeans, a blazer, and scuffed loafers, or a T-shirt and motorcycle boots. At all times, he wears a gold Rolex "President" watch. In person, he has a sociable nature and a roguish charm and comes across like the kind of guy you might encounter late at night in a barroom, jive-talking one of the waitresses. As a bandleader, however, he is mercurial and governs by mood. He once threatened to fire the rhythm guitarist because his hair had grown beyond appropriate Ron Wood length. On the other hand, when he's having a good time, and particularly when he's been drinking, he will climb behind the drum kit, to the frustration of more authentic-minded band members. "Who ever heard of Mick Jagger playing the drums?" the drummer once remarked, exasperated. Glen is equally contradictory in appraising his own talents, swinging between modesty and extreme boastfulness. "I know what it's like to walk in Mick's shoes—with lift supports, mind you," he once told me. He has also told me, "If you want me to go out and front a band, I'll do it as good as maybe ten other guys in the world can do it."

In fact, Sticky Fingers has had considerable success. The band, which is based in the New York–New Jersey area, travels all over the country, performing at rock clubs, bars, biker rallies, birthdays and weddings, casinos, corporate events, and colleges, being especially popular at fraternity houses in the South, where

Sticky Fingers has become a fixture of Greek life, as indelible as keg stands and hazing. A few years ago, Sticky Fingers flew to Rotterdam, Netherlands, to appear at a "tribute fest" in the Ahoy arena and performed along with other tribute bands in front of eleven thousand people. Bruce Springsteen played the same venue the following night. Most engagements, however, are less glamorous. Tribute bands occupy the lower rungs of the show-business ladder, somewhere between lounge bands and wedding singers, and even a successful act like Sticky Fingers leads a schizophrenic existence. I spent a year hanging out with the band members, and for every Ahoy arena, there were a dozen times when they drove hundreds of miles to play at a tiny bar or frat house, spent the night in a cheap motel or none at all, and returned home with neither wealth nor glory. Such experiences never dampened their enthusiasm to go back out and play again.

For most people, tribute bands are a hobby, a chance to assume the role of the musical heroes of their youth. But Glen is the rare tribute performer who has turned being someone else into a full-time endeavor, and in conversation he gives the impression he's spent the past decade sharing a tour bus with the Marshall Tucker Band. He speaks in the animated, slangy palaver of an FM disc jockey and uses words like *gig* and *backline*. Describing a former drummer, he says, "Tightest pocket I've ever heard—cat could play reggae like only the natives can." He carries himself like an old-hand rock star, too; when I visited him at home, he drove me around in a Mercedes convertible while drinking a vodka-cranberry from a rocks glass. From habit, he occasionally slipped into a British accent. It's difficult not to experience confusion between his dual lives: in his role as Mick Jagger, he has signed autographs, posed for pictures, been flown around the world, attracted beautiful women, appeared in magazines and on television. Returning home he is met with obscurity. As he likes to say, "Here's this average guy who pays his cable bill and takes out the trash like everyone else, but he gets to experience some of what it's like to be a rock star." When he says this, I often smile to myself; *average guy* does not come to mind when I think of Glen.

I first met Glen Carroll a few years ago, when a magazine I was working for at the time was planning a music issue and I suggested an article about tribute bands. Tribute bands might seem a lightweight subject, but on closer examination they reveal semi-serious things about our culture: our celebrity worship, the baby boomer nostalgia that pervades modern entertainment, the seeming exhaustion of new ideas in art, film, fashion, music. In fact, the essential notion of a tribute band—that is, something directly inspired by what has gone before—extends beyond music to the entire culture. Stephen Colbert is, in a way, a tribute band to Bill O'Reilly. Quentin Tarantino is a tribute band to 1970s blaxploitation and B movies. You could think of Dita Von Teese as a tribute band to the fifties sex symbol Bettie Page. Gus Van Sant's shot-for-shot remake of *Psycho* is unquestionably a tribute band to the Alfred Hitchcock original. Karaoke is based on the same premise as a tribute band, as is the popular video game Guitar Hero, in which players replicate, note for note, famous guitar solos.

Tribute bands are indicative of the desire for easy fame without accomplishment because their lure is this: by putting on a black wig and a top hat, you can become Slash from Guns N'

Roses, a guitar god. Most tribute performers either dreamed of being rock stars but ended up working more mundane jobs instead or they actually pursued a career in music that didn't work out. Maybe they were talented, but not talented enough. Or maybe they formed a roots-rock band and wrote earnest songs about the heartland and, in search of a record deal, moved to Hollywood in 1985, right around the time the record companies were signing the flashy hair-metal bands. Playing in a tribute band offers a second chance to experience stardom, however refracted. It is basically wish fulfillment—the rock and roll equivalent of those fantasy baseball camps where grown men suit up and take the field and bat balls around, something I've always found a little melancholy, but sort of endearing, too.

Something else I find appealing about tribute bands is that they are unabashed believers in rock and roll, at a time when the form appears to have hit a dry spell. Record sales have declined for the past decade. Legendary rock clubs like CBGB have closed. Video games, the Internet, and cable TV all compete with music for primacy in the teenage head. And technology and changing times are eliminating many of the tribal rites surrounding rock and roll. I once listened to a fairly famous drummer who had grown up on Long Island in the seventies talk fondly of camping on line to buy concert tickets to see The Who. Halfway through the conversation, I realized Ticketmaster.com had made that custom completely irrelevant. In the same way, the iPod is making irrelevant the full-length album, the album cover, the ritual of studying liner notes, the midnight record store sale, and, eventually, the record store itself. New rituals will develop, of course. But at a tribute show, classic rock culture reigns in all its high-decibel glory. I think of tribute bands as being like those historical reenactors, dressing up and reliving a golden age of rock and roll—a time before the commercial dominance of pop and hip-hop, before DJs replaced live bands, before radio and record company conglomeration, before things like guitar solos and groupies and rock operas became ironic. A great number of tribute musicians belong to this time; they grew up in the seventies and eighties reading *Circus* and *Creem* and hanging posters of Jimmy Page and Randy Rhoads on their bedroom wall, and they saw bands like KISS and Black Sabbath in concert long before the reunion tours. Although I am a decade younger, I feel I belong to this time, too. I mostly listen to seventies rock bands like Mott the Hoople and Thin Lizzy and the Faces. I watch a lot of VH1 Classic. I've had long and involved conversations about the guitar tones on Robin Trower's *Bridge of Sighs* album. Also, I don't own an iPod, or a CD player, or a tape deck, but listen instead to LPs, which puts me four technologies behind the times. Basically, I'm an analog kind of guy. In this way, I share with tribute musicians a longing for the rock music of an earlier time and a sense of displacement in the modern music scene.

For the magazine story, I picked a few tribute bands that sounded intriguing—an all-girl tribute to AC/DC called AC/DShe; an ABBA band, Björn Again; the Atomic Punks, a Van Halen tribute from Hollywood; and Hysteria, a tribute to Def Leppard from West Warwick, Rhode Island (New England, oddly, is a tribute band hotbed). I picked Sticky Fingers because I love the music of the Rolling Stones and because I think in their prime Mick Jagger and Keith Richards were the coolest people walking the planet. When I called the number on the Sticky Fingers Web site, I found myself speaking to a woman in New Jersey named Kerry Muldoon, who was acting as the band's manager.

Sticky Fingers didn't have any upcoming shows, but Kerry said I could interview Glen. And so one Saturday in June 2001 I drove from my home in Brooklyn to Massachusetts, where Glen was living at the time.

Glen's house was in South Dartmouth, a white colonial on a quiet street that sloped down to the bay. When I arrived, around noon, he answered the door and made a big show of inviting me in. "Don't worry about the signs," he said, motioning to several NO TRESPASSING signs nailed to the porch. "I've got a low-level stalker." That day, he wore a slim-fitting black shirt, black straight-legged jeans, and loafers, sort of rocker-casual. I'd seen pictures of him on the band's Web site but was taken aback by how much he resembled Mick Jagger in person, especially in his build, which was slight and wiry. I had the peculiar feeling all afternoon of being in the presence of a celebrity I'd never heard of.

Glen led me through a front room that contained a well-stocked liquor cabinet, then down into a sunken living room. The interior was well appointed: stuffed chairs, antique dark-wood furniture, acres of molding. On one wall hung a framed photo of Glen onstage at the Montreal Spectrum; another showed him backstage at a concert with the albino keyboard player Edgar Winter. On a bookshelf were more photos and some books about the Rolling Stones. Glen fixed himself a cocktail. Looking through a picture window whose view took in his neighbors and the bay, he said, "These houses were built with whaling money," and gave the name of an obscure sea captain who, he said, had owned his home. Then he said, "We've got another home right down on Water Street that we may move into, but it's smaller than this place and not as good for entertaining." He was referring to his girlfriend or his wife—it wasn't clear which. Her name was Julia.

She was blond and petite, and pretty in a fragile sort of way, like a porcelain doll. She had laid out a vegetable plate when we first entered the living room, then disappeared into the recesses of the house, the way some women do when their men have guests over.

"Why did you decide to sing in a tribute band?" I asked.

"Why can one band be flown to Moscow, while another one can't get out of town?" Glen said. "Why is it that some doctors make nothing as a general practitioner and a heart surgeon makes five hundred thousand dollars a year? They're specialists. People hire me to do something that I specialize in. I just did the holiday party for the city of Charleston this past New Year's. It was at the Civic Center. There were five thousand people there. And they *loved* it." He swirled his drink. "For a show like that, I had to go out there with the mainstream stuff, the standards," he said. "But I do things, too, where the audience has to be fans to get it. We'll be doing 'Midnight Rambler,' that live '72 style. Oh man! I've got the belt and I slam it down onstage. Then during 'Satisfaction,' I'll tell the boys to throw in a few bars of Led Zeppelin or 'Day Tripper.' The people go mad. Like Keith Richards said, there's only one song."

Over the course of the afternoon (and several vodka-cranberries), Glen told me of his adventures in music. He was an engaging, if unfocused, storyteller. Like country roads, his stories tended to follow a confusing and eccentric geography. He illustrated one anecdote about moving to Los Angeles in 1978 to play music by showing me a classified ad seeking musicians that he'd placed in a 1987 issue of *Rolling Stone.* The cocktails didn't act as a clarifier. Still, you couldn't say he wasn't entertaining. I heard about the time he showed up at Ron Wood's gated mansion in Los Angeles and rang the buzzer and spoke to the maid (Woody wasn't home); and about the time Sticky Fingers played a gig at the Toy Tiger in Louisville, Kentucky, and Gilby Clarke of Guns N' Roses sat in with the band and then afterward everyone partied with the Coors girls; and the occasion he met Leslie West of Mountain backstage at a concert and Leslie had been a "real prick." Julia popped into the room several times; she and Glen jokingly referred to me as "the Enemy," the nickname the press-wary rock band gives the journalist character in the Cameron Crowe movie *Almost Famous.* But Glen wasn't at all guarded; on the contrary, he talked at length and without restraint, as if he'd been waiting his whole life for someone like me to show up.

At one point, he motioned me over to a bookcase whose shelves were lined with CDs, videos, and bootleg concert tapes, all of the Rolling Stones. "My homework," he said. The Stones have been recording together continuously since 1963, and their output is substantial: twenty-five studio albums, eight live records, a boxed set of singles and B sides, several rarities collections—a vast reservoir of songs that encompasses blues, rock, reggae, country, psychedelic, and disco that would take months to fully listen to. The band's catalog is so deep that entire albums can go overlooked. For instance, *Goats Head Soup* was released in 1973 and is mostly ignored by casual fans but contains a beautiful ballad ("Winter") and an odd but moving song about heroin addiction sung by Keith Richards ("Coming Down Again") and a hit single, "Angie." One of my favorite Stones songs is a track on *Sticky Fingers* called "Sway." It opens with a thunderous riff, like something you'd hear on a Black Sabbath record, and has a sweeping chorus whose refrain is "It's just that demon life has got you in its sway." Every time I hear it, I want to get up and *move*. Mick Jagger has probably forgotten he wrote it.

Glen owned every Stones album I'd ever heard and several that I hadn't. "You would not believe the Stones stuff I have," he said excitedly. "I have stuff that Jagger's maid sends me out of his closets. This is the special remake, Don Was–produced twelve-minute version of 'Out of Tears.' . . . Do you know about the *Ned Kelly* sound track? . . . Here's an early version of 'Tumbling Dice.' " Of his affection for the Stones, he said, "It started when I was six years old. I was in a skating rink in Marietta, Georgia. The DJ said, 'We have a new song from the Rolling Stones called "Satisfaction." ' I heard that *dunt, dunt, da-da-da.* It was the hook!"

Glen was born in Springfield, Massachusetts, in 1960. His father was a career soldier in the air force, and while Glen was growing up, he and his parents and his younger sister lived all over the world. For part of Glen's teens, his father was stationed in England, and when the Rolling Stones played Earls Court, in London, in 1976, Glen and a classmate ditched school to go. It was the first of the band's tours that were less rock concerts than traveling spectacles: the stage unfolded like a lotus flower to reveal the band members, and during the show an inflatable phallus emerged from the floor. The night made a deep impression on Glen. It suggested the possibility of a grand life by becoming a rock star. A year later, the family moved again, to Summerville, South Carolina, near Charleston. By then, Glen had taken up the drums and was playing in local bands, performing at backyard parties and beer bashes in the woods. He wanted to be a musician, but he eventually enlisted in the military, in part to please his father, and spent eleven years flying and working on aircraft in the air force and army.

Glen walked over to the bookshelf, took out an old leather-bound scrapbook, and sat back down. Pasted to the first page was a backstage pass from a ZZ Top concert on the *Eliminator* tour. Most of the photos in the book were of Glen's cars—Corvettes and Dodge Challengers polished and gleaming in the sun—or former girlfriends. The girls all had feathered hair, like Farrah Fawcett. "Oh, my DeLorean," he remarked fondly upon seeing one photo. "For a blowhead in the eighties, what other car could you want?" On another page was a newspaper clipping from the *Berkeley Democrat* in Moncks Corner, South Carolina, dated March 25, 1981. The first paragraph read: "Berkeley County's latest and perhaps best nightspot has recently opened in Moncks Corner. The Duckblind, operated by 'Will' Sellers and 'Chico' Cartagena, is located in the same building known previously as Bart's or the Moncks Corner Pool Room on Hwy. 52." Farther down, it said: "Debuting at the club Friday night was FINAL NOTICE. This was the first professional play date of the five-member board. The group has been together about six weeks but they play like they have been together for years. Glen Carroll, from Summerville, is a ROLLING STONES fan. As the drummer, he plays hard and clean rhythms, acting like the glue which holds the pieces together."

Glen said, "I kept getting many, many bills. Electric bill—final notice. Water bill—final notice. Hey guys, I've got a name for the band!" As he flipped through the pages, more stories unfolded: "This is a Rolling Stones show, Tangerine Bowl. This is the girl I went with, Shannon Hall. A beautiful woman. We dated for years. . . . This is when I was flying in the military. I was stationed in Ozark, Alabama, and me and these cats put together a band called the Ozark Swamp Aviators for a talent show. That's my stick buddy Steve 'Mad Max' Lomax on guitar. . . . This is in L.A., outside the Whisky A Go-Go. I was in a Stones band called Black and Blue. I was changing bands like underwear. . . ." By now, it was getting late. I stayed for another hour, during which time Glen played me some songs he'd written for an original album he planned to release. "I want to use Edgar Winter on the album. I want to use Chuck Leavell. Rick Derringer, I know I can get," he said as a catchy rocker he wrote called "Pull In, Pull Out" played. "There will be Rolling Stones chops, but it won't sound like a rip-off record. It'll sound like a guy who went to Rock and Roll 101." I promised Glen I would go to see Sticky Fingers perform sometime, then drove back to New York.

On Monday, back at work, I received an unexpected call from Julia. "I wanted to clear a few things up," she said in a tentative and apologetic tone, then went on to explain that Glen had gotten carried away and that he didn't own the house I visited, as he'd led me to believe. It belonged to her and her husband, from whom she was separating. The husband was living nearby, in the home that Glen had described as too small for entertaining. Julia asked me not to mention the house in my story, because Glen wasn't supposed to be living there and it might affect her divorce proceedings. I said I would keep that part out of the article.

I didn't see Glen for a few years after that. It wasn't ill will. You can't get mad at a guy pretending to be Mick Jagger for bullshitting you a little. Later, after I got to know him, I came to see

Glen not as a plain liar but as someone who approached the truth like a set designer, rearranging a fact here and sprucing up a detail there to present a version of life as he believed it should be. I imagine the idea of him and Julia owning that old colonial together was preferable to the messier reality.

One day, in early 2005, I got to thinking about that afternoon in Massachusetts and found Glen through the Sticky Fingers Web site. He was living in northern New Jersey now, in the town of Little Falls. In the years since I'd seen him last, he and Julia must have split up, because when I drove out there one January evening, I was met at the door by a woman named Lara, who was blond and doting like Julia but not as pretty. They shared a brick town house in a condo development full of identical brick town houses, and the interior had the mixed furnishings and crowded appearance common when two people's lives come together quickly. The living room was dominated by Glen's sound equipment; near the door was a computer, where he spent his time attending to the business of Sticky Fingers: contacting agents and promoters, booking shows, making travel plans, and updating the band's Web site, which is a marvel of suggestive marketing. It includes a brief and complimentary history of the band and a "References" page that lists famous acts Sticky Fingers has shared the bill with like Alice Cooper and Foghat, venues the band has performed in like Mustang Sally's in Little Rock, Arkansas, and, curiously, "The First Lady and Governor of Tennessee." A "Friends of the Band" link contains candid snapshots of, among other things, Glen hanging out with "good friend" Les Paul, Glen shaking hands with former Super Bowl MVP Marcus Allen before a gig at a golf tournament, and an autographed publicity photo of Cher, which reads, "To Glen, Love Ya Babe Cher." Owing to the notoriously high turnover rate in bands, there is also an "Employment" section containing perhaps the first-ever job application to grace a rock group's Web site. (Sample question: "Do you have dependable transportation?")

That night, Glen was in an upbeat mood because he'd recently returned from playing a charity gala in Atlanta. Ted Turner founded the charity, and Ted and Jane Fonda attended the party. Glen told me that Jane was "lovely" in person. I was skeptical, given our previous encounter, but he showed me a photo of the two of them taken at the event; in the photo, Glen was practically sitting on Jane Fonda's lap.

Sticky Fingers had gone international in the intervening years. The band had performed in Panama, and from a poster hanging in the living room, I saw there had been a weeklong residence at a Hard Rock Hotel in Bali, Indonesia. Glen said the coming year was shaping up to be his best yet. The band had a new Keith—a guy from Chicago, whom Glen described as "the best Keith I've ever played with. As good a Keith as I am a Mick." The Rolling Stones were finishing a new album, to be released later that year, and talk was swirling that they would be launching a world tour. For a tribute band, this was like winning the lottery. Radio stations would put Stones songs in heavy rotation and Mick Jagger and Keith Richards would appear in magazines and on TV, rousing fans. Like remora, the little feeder fish that accompany sharks, Sticky Fingers would follow the Stones from city to city, playing radio station promotions and preconcert parties at bars and rock clubs wherever the tour passed through. "When Charlie beat cancer, I was so excited," Glen said, referring to the band's drummer, Charlie Watts, and sounding as thrilled for Charlie as he was for himself.

I was intrigued by Glen's curious form of celebrity, the way he had achieved a degree of renown through the renown of another person. I wondered what, if any, psychological effects there were in pretending to be someone. And what about the Rolling Stones? Were they aware that another band was going around pretending to be them?

Not long after that evening with Glen in New Jersey, I decided to follow Sticky Fingers as they followed the Stones, with the notion that by viewing a copy in relation to the real thing it would bring the tribute world into relief, in the way placing a black silhouette against a white background defines its form. Eventually, I talked to other musicians and spent time with other groups, to find the reasons why tribute bands were so popular and to discover if watching a copy of your favorite band is in some ways more rewarding than watching the actual band. And so one weekend in the spring of 2005, I went on the road with Sticky Fingers.

The band was booked to play the Sigma Chi fraternity house at Hampden-Sydney College, near Farmville, Virginia. Like most working bands, Sticky Fingers has performed in every type of venue imaginable and before every type of crowd, but fraternities, especially fraternities in the South, where there is a long tradition of hiring rock and R&B bands to entertain at parties, remain its natural milieu. At a frat party, where hundreds of coeds are stuffed into a room, chugging cheap beer, the songs of the Stones, loose and sexual, celebrate a lifestyle.

That morning, the band's drummer, Dan Gorgone, picked me up at my apartment in Brooklyn. Aside from his role as Charlie Watts, whom he doesn't really resemble, Dan had lately been doubling as the band's road manager, ferrying members and gear in his Isuzu Trooper. Dan is forty-nine. He is tall and broad-shouldered, with brown, dry-look-style hair, glasses, and a formality to his speech uncharacteristic to rock musicians. When I got in the car, he greeted me by saying, "According to MapQuest, this drive is seven hours. I picked you up at nine-thirty A.M. We should arrive a little after five P.M., barring any traffic problems."

On the drive, Dan told me about himself, explaining that he grew up in the West Village and now lived with his wife and three-year-old daughter in Flushing, Queens. For many years, he said, he worked on Wall Street as a money manager, but after some bad moves during the dot-com bust, he lost several clients and wound up working construction. Two years earlier, on a job site, a power saw had cut his arm and he received a disability settlement, which he was living on while playing music on the side.

As we headed south on I-95 through New Jersey, I looked around Dan's car. The inside was fastidiously neat. A cell phone was clipped to the dash. CDs were tucked into overhead visor pockets; one of them was a mix he'd made for his wife's fortieth birthday that included the Beatles song "Michelle"—his wife's name. A Sticky Fingers key chain dangled from the ignition, and hanging from a hook in the backseat was a dry-cleaning bag with his Charlie outfit: black dress slacks and a maroon button-up shirt.

It was clear that Dan derived great pleasure from his role in Sticky Fingers. "When you get on the road with your band, there's nothing like it in the world," he said. "You have fun. You trade stories. When I tell the guys I play basketball with that I'm traveling to Sigma Chi fraternity to play for twenty-two-year-old girls, they treat me like I'm *in* the Rolling Stones."

I asked him how his wife looked upon these weekends

on the road. "To be perfectly honest, it's not always the easiest thing," he said. "But if we have family obligations and there's a Sticky Fingers show, I say, 'Honey, you'll have to go alone. I'm gigging.' "

Dan exited the interstate in southern New Jersey, drove a mile up the highway, and pulled into the parking lot of a chain hotel. He drove to the back of the lot and parked alongside a rusty Chevrolet Celebrity; in the driver's seat was George Steckert, the band's bassist. Earlier, I had asked Dan to describe George, and he had said, "George is a stalwart, a true musician." George is thirty-eight, tall, good-looking, with long brown hair, a ruddy complexion, and an affable, surfer-dude manner. He lives on the Jersey shore, where he works odd jobs, surfs, and rides his bike. That day, he was wearing what he often wore on road trips—a pair of dark jeans, a leather jacket, and imitation python shoes.

"Okay, ramblers," George said, loading his amplifier into Dan's car, "let's ramble."

As it happened, the band was currently between Ron Woods, and the new Keith couldn't make the show because he hadn't accrued any vacation time at his job, so Glen had hired fill-in guitarists for the night, who were meeting us at the show. (Glen was driving up from central Florida, where his parents had retired to and where he was considering moving.) According to Dan, I was missing out because the new Keith took a Method approach to the role.

"He *is* Keith, right down to the Rebel Yell, twenty-years-of-smoking rasp," Dan said. "If anything, he's *too* Keith, the Keith that needed blood transfusions and had to be propped up onstage."

"Oh man," George said. "We're in the airport, and he's walking around like Keith does with all that shit in his hair. He's got, like, his car keys in there."

"He's the Keithiest Keith," Dan said.

"The Keithiest," George agreed.

The drive was like most interstate drives, long and uneventful, except for one moment in Virginia when we were pulled over by a policeman for speeding. By then, we were on a two-lane road not far from the college and George was behind the wheel. His license, a temporary one, had no photo and looked vaguely phony. He also had marijuana in his coat pocket. In an effort to placate the patrolman, Dan leaned toward the driver's side window and said, "We're in a band and we're on our way to a show, officer. We're Sticky Fingers." The policeman was unmoved. But after he ran George's license and it came back okay, he let us go with a warning. When he was gone, and we were back on the highway, we laughed in relief and talked about what a close call it had been and imagined less fortunate outcomes the rest of the way.

The Sigma Chi fraternity is in a small and deceptively tidy-looking Georgian-style house on a leafy street in the center of the Hampden-Sydney campus. When we arrived, in the early evening, a group of fraternity brothers dressed in polo shirts, their collars upturned, were standing on the patio, drinking beer. Hampden-Sydney is a private school for men (George had been calling it "Homo Sydney" all day), but girls had been bused in for the night from a nearby women's college, and they stood around nervously. "Baby Hold On" by Eddie Money pumped from the speakers of the neighboring frat house.

Glen and the substitute players hadn't yet arrived, so George and I fished bottles of Budweiser out of a plastic cooler and stood on the patio while Dan went off to find the frat brother in charge. The sky was in the last traces of daylight, and the air was cold and damp. The lawn surrounding the Sigma Chi house was a muddy mess; beer cans and litter were strewn everywhere. There were also a disconcerting number of police cars driving up and down Fraternity Row, and campus cops patrolling on foot.

A skinny guy with a brush mustache wearing a NASCAR T-shirt walked over and introduced himself as the soundman for the show. I asked him why there were so many cops.

"It's Greek Week," he said, and looked down at the ground, which was covered with glass shards from beer bottles that had been broken on the cement patio. "I tell you, these fucking kids love to break glass," the soundman said. "That's my pet peeve. It gets in the cords of my equipment. That shit'll be on your feet, in your shoes. You'll be picking it off you for a week." He shook his head and gave one of those "I was young once, too" laughs. "Oh boy, you watch. They'll go wild tonight."

George walked inside the house to the band's dressing area, which was no more than a frat brother's messy bedroom, and plopped down on a chair and began watching a TV show about Paris Hilton. Awhile later, Dan came into the room looking worried. "I just met the guitar players. The Keith doesn't sing," he said gravely. "This is the first Keith I've played with who doesn't sing. We can't do 'Happy' or 'T&A.' "

George followed Dan back out to the frat's party space—a bunkerlike room off the patio, constructed entirely of concrete, as if built to withstand great punishment. The fill-in guitarists were on a plywood stage, tinkering with their amplifiers. One guy had strawberry-blond hair and pink skin, while the other, the Keith, looked like a friendly dad. Neither resembled any member of the Stones.

There was an exchange of small talk among Dan, George, and the guitarists, who had driven from Philadelphia, where they played in their own Stones band, Shattered. After a moment, Dan pulled his stage outfit from the dry-cleaning bag. "So," he said, addressing the substitute Keith, whose name was Eric Senderoff, "do you want to go into a closet and get into character? I mean, you know, are you going to get Keithed up?"

Eric was dressed in jeans and a floral shirt. "This is it," he said. "I am Keithed up."

Dan looked dumbfounded. The whole point of the evening—indeed the very existence of Sticky Fingers—seemed to be called into question. Is a Stones tribute band without a guitarist who looks like Keith Richards still a Stones tribute band?

"Glen called me up and said he needed two guitar players for tonight," Eric said. "He knows we don't do the whole look-alike thing."

"I don't see the point," the other guitarist said. "I don't look anything like the Stones."

"I've never played a show like this," Dan said, recovering from his initial shock, "and I love you guys and can tell you're great players. But I'm going to put on black slacks because that's what Charlie wears."

Just then, there was a commotion in the doorway and Glen appeared. He was wearing a white blazer over a white oxford shirt, stonewashed jeans, and scuffed brown loafers, and he strode into the room with the casual entitlement of a fifth-year senior.

Casting his eyes around, he declared, "Greek Week," as if he were an expert on the rituals of university life, then added, "Oh man, wait until you see the University of Alabama in September!"

A good-looking blonde walked over to Glen and asked if she could have her picture taken with him. He posed dutifully. More girls gathered at his side. "Will you play 'Can't You Hear Me Knocking'?" one asked sweetly.

"Don't hold me to it, but maybe," Glen said.

At 9:30 P.M., Glen lit a cigarette, climbed onstage, and instructed the band to run through a sound check. "Okay, Sweet Virginia," he said to the crowd after the band played a number, "we'll be back in a few minutes with the Stones show for y'all."

When the band returned fifteen minutes later, Glen had changed into a skintight yellow shirt and black trousers. The lights darkened and the room tensed and filled with coeds. As soon as Sticky Fingers hit the opening chords of "Honky Tonk Women," the crowd erupted, yelling and dancing, guzzling beer and spilling just as much on the cement floor. The pressure in the room seemed to build intensely and release in bursts, like waves crashing on a beach. The song's familiar chorus swelled and the audience sang: "IT'S A HAW-O-ONG, HAW-O-ONG-KEE TONK WOMEN! GIMME, GIMME, GIMME THE HONKY TONK BLUUUUUUES."

I stood in the back of the room, near the soundman, who was simultaneously working the board and safeguarding his equipment against stray beer suds, and watched Sticky Fingers work. Glen is, by his own admission, not a gifted singer, but he is a charismatic performer, and onstage he moved in a highly entertaining retrospective of Mick Jagger's signature moves: the petulant hand-on-the-hip, the show-pony prance, the full-lipped pout and cocksure strut. At one point, he singled out "the girl in front with the 34D's" for a song request, and later, two big blondes jumped onstage with the band and began gyrating in time to the beat. Glen dirty-danced alongside them and the girls giggled.

"All right, Sweet Virginia," Glen yelled to the crowd, "let me hear you. . . ."

2

Glen Carroll is not the founder of Sticky Fingers, although most people assume otherwise, and he does not often correct them. The group was formed in 1981 in New Jersey by a music manager who represented a talented but foundering show band called Sam the Band. To keep them from breaking up, the manager suggested Sam the Band become a tribute to the Stones, who were touring at the time, and he decided on the name Sticky Fingers, after the title of the band's 1971 album, and also for the slightly lurid connotation. The original Mick was a flamboyant singer named Larry Larue, who liked to arrive at concerts in a limousine. In the eighties, tribute bands were still a novelty, and for many years Sticky Fingers traveled up and down the East Coast, performing four or five nights a week to mesmerized crowds. By 1988 musical tastes had shifted, the crowds disappeared, and Larry

Larue eventually left music to open a hair salon in New Jersey. This is when Glen entered the picture.

Glen was discharged from the military in 1989 and moved with his then wife to Suffield, Connecticut, where he worked for a company that supplied airplane parts. He was bored and discontented and decided to try music again, approaching the idea with a trademark mix of outsize optimism, practicality, and shrewdness. "There are different levels of bands," he once explained. "There are local bands, and by 'local,' I mean bands that will play within an hour or so from home. Then there are regional bands and national bands. 'National' means you can get out to California, you can get down to Florida or Texas. I had it in my mind to be an international band. I went around the world when I was a kid and I didn't want to play in front of local yokels the rest of my life. The only way I could see it happening, other than getting a record contract—which I wasn't finding under my pillow each morning—was to emulate something that would have a worldwide demand."

According to Glen, he settled on the name Sticky Fingers, unaware of the earlier version, and placed a classified ad in a local newspaper seeking musicians for a Stones tribute. When a former guitarist in Larry Larue's band contacted him, Glen became the new singer of the old Sticky Fingers. I have heard differing versions of the story that suggest Glen simply revived the name, the way a clever businessman might resurrect an old-school sneaker brand to capitalize on its storied reputation. At first, Glen drummed, and the band was fronted by a singer ill suited for the role. "The guy didn't look anything like Mick Jagger—he just looked like a woman," Tom Guerra, one of the band's early guitarists, told me. "We'd be playing a biker bar and he'd come out wearing blue mascara and a little white dress." Everyone who saw the band in those years thought Glen should be the singer because, even with short hair, he bore a remarkable resemblance to Mick Jagger. But Glen had never been a singer before, and he was insecure about his voice, so he asked Tom Guerra to record a sort of karaoke tape of Stones music for him to practice over. He'd been laid off from his job and, at twenty-nine, was delivering newspapers for money. For a year, he drove around Connecticut delivering papers and singing Stones songs—*"It's the Hoonnk-eeee Tonk, Hoonnk-eeee Tonk Women!"*—behind the wheel of his car.

From the moment Glen became the singer of Sticky Fingers, his focus was getting out on the road. His enthusiasm for touring was tireless and wide-ranging: bars, rock clubs, boardwalks, fairgrounds—the venue didn't matter, nor did the distances traveled to get there. Glen would drive the band halfway across the country for a one-nighter, then turn around and drive straight home, a grueling schedule he still maintains. "Twenty-two hours in a van with five guys—I don't care how good your deodorant is," Dan Gorgone said of a trip to Mississippi. Southern universities in particular became a favored destination. Sticky Fingers are legends in the frat houses of Alabama, Georgia, Tennessee, and Louisiana, and perform so frequently in Virginia that the band once showed up at the *right* fraternity chapter in the *wrong* college town. ("Man, the promoter had a hard time understanding that one," Glen said.) Occasionally, the band established a residency at a particular venue, like the Rock 'n' Roll Café, a bar on Bleecker Street in Greenwich Village that was a sort of Fillmore East for tribute bands until it closed sometime around 2000. Sticky Fingers held a monthly residency, and performed there on New Year's Eve as well for a group of Stones superfans who call themselves the Shidoobees. But mostly, the band traveled. On the road, they were often mistaken for a more famous group.

"Y'all are a band, aren't you?" a waitress at a Cracker Barrel once asked them. "Are y'all Froghat?"

"Yes, that's right," Glen told her. "We are Froghat."

This sort of overheated touring schedule is common to bands trying to attract the interest of a record label, or promote an album, but it's rare for a tribute band, which by definition has a limited career trajectory. Unlike most tribute performers, though, Glen views singing in Sticky Fingers not as a pastime but as a full-time occupation. Keeping a working band together and on the road for eighteen years is no small achievement. Musicians are by nature temperamental and prone to fleeting associations. This is especially true in tribute bands, where there aren't strong incentives—like contractual obligations or the lure of fame—for the members to stick together through disagreements. Also, it's difficult to find someone willing or able to go to Russia for a week, or drive to Alabama over Fourth of July weekend.

As a result, Glen runs Sticky Fingers less like a typical band—that is, a fixed set of musicians who perform together on a regular basis—and more in the style of a cost-cutting CEO, outsourcing for players. There are Charlie Wattses and Ronnie Woods and Bill Wymans scattered from Florida to Tennessee. A guy might play in the band for a year, drift out of the picture, then return; another might do one show and disappear forever. The same lineup is rarely together more than a few months. Former members turn up all over. I once saw an Aerosmith tribute band called Draw the Line at a Princeton University eating club and thought the Joe Perry looked strangely familiar—and then realized he'd been Ron Wood in Sticky Fingers.

In fact, an astonishing number of musicians have passed through Sticky Fingers over the years. I once tried to count them all but gave up somewhere around forty-six. There have been close to twenty Keiths alone. One of the first was Gar Francis, who also played in the original version of Sticky Fingers with Larry Larue. Another Keith was Daniel Hoffenberg, a slightly built Frenchman who mastered Richards's trademark open-tuning guitar style, which Richards himself once described as requiring "five strings, three chords, two fingers, and one asshole." Daniel Hoffenberg's father was Mason Hoffenberg, who, with Terry Southern, cowrote the novel *Candy* and hung around with Bob Dylan and the Band in Woodstock. Johnny Shoe Polish was a Keith, so named for his habit of applying black shoe polish to his scalp to approximate Richards's ashen look. Another guitarist was so chronically broke he made salads from the fixings bar at interstate truck stops. At one point, the Charlie Watts was Japanese, and the Bill Wyman was a woman. In the year I spent with Sticky Fingers, no fewer than four bassists passed through the band, including Angello Olivieri, a Brooklyn native with a towering pompadour hairdo that is positively architectural. A number of Sticky Fingers alumni are semiprofessional musicians, like Hal B. Selzer, a well-known bassist on the Jersey rock scene who sometimes backs the R&B singer Gary U.S. Bonds. Hal also arranged for his old friend Jon Bon Jovi to duet with Sticky Fingers when the band played the Borgata Casino in Atlantic City. And a few former members are semifamous: Kenny Aaronson, another bassist, played on Rick Derringer's records in the seventies and toured with Bob Dylan; Bobby Chouinard, a big, garrulous guy who drummed for Billy Squier and lived the rock-star life to the hilt, performed with Sticky Fingers toward the end of his life, before he died of a heart attack, in 1997, at age forty-three.

Glen's method of assembling a band could be described as improvisational. If he needs a substitute musician, he flips through his Rolodex and makes calls until he finds someone who is available; short a drummer, he once enlisted a girlfriend's teenage son. If he were paying tribute to any other band, he would probably have run aground years ago, but the Stones' music allows for, perhaps even fosters, a loose approach. Tom Guerra, the guitarist who first encouraged Glen to sing, and who now plays in his own original band, the Mambo Sons, told me, "The Stones' music is all based on feel, and it's based on the blues, and the other thing is that the Stones are so mainstream that every musician knows those songs and knows the arrangements. I don't think somebody could walk into a Zeppelin tribute band without any rehearsal and play the entire night unless they were a Zeppelin freak. With the Stones, you find out what key it's in, and by the end of the song you basically have it figured out. But the saving grace is that nobody is ever going to see Sticky Fingers and say they were sloppy, because the Stones are sloppy when they play live."

To replenish his stable of musicians Glen periodically runs classified ads and holds auditions, which is how Dan Gorgone came to join the band. Dan said, "This was in 1999. I hadn't drummed for two years and I picked up the *Village Voice* one week and saw the ad. I went to the audition, which was in a rehearsal studio in Manhattan, and met Kerry. Daniel was there and I looked around and said, 'I'm pretty sure I see the guy who's the Keith Richards, but where's the Mick?' Kerry said, 'He'll be here, but he's going to be late.' If I recall, we played 'Brown Sugar';

then we played 'Sympathy.' After a half hour, in bops Glen with some guy who called himself Stewart and who looked just like Rod Stewart. Julia was with him, too, and I remember she was wearing a fur and looked impressive. Glen came in like a real rock star, with the shades, strutting in, the blazer—the whole thing. I said to myself, Maybe this isn't some rinky-dink outfit. Maybe this is something big."

Dan told me that story on the way to Hampden-Sydney, and when I asked him why one guy or another was no longer in the band, he often replied, "Well, he and Glen had a falling-out." It was a common refrain, and seemed to explain, in part, why the band never maintained internal stability. One former band member I spoke to described Glen as "a complicated personality," by which he meant that he was capable of being mean, spiteful, vainglorious, and manipulative, and, in turn, generous, kind, insightful, and funny. Dan said, "I've seen Glen be the most charming person in the world or the schoolboy in disgrace." As it turned out, this was Dan's second stint in Sticky Fingers; the first ended with him quitting after an argument with Glen over the band's direction. During the argument, Glen had called Dan the worst drummer he ever played with. A year later, Glen called and asked him if he would like to do some shows in the New York area. Dan said, "I thought I was the worst drummer you've ever played with."

"No," Glen said, "I've played with several worse since you."

Some band members had disagreed with Glen over what they regarded as his ragtag approach to running a band—the way he used "pick-up" musicians and never held rehearsals, so that musical growth was impossible. Mostly, though, people seemed bothered by Glen's drinking, which was frequent and generally excessive. Bartenders marveled at the amount of liquor he could consume, but consumption was by no means limited to a barroom. Talking to him on the phone, I could sometimes hear the tinkling of ice in a rocks glass and detect a dark undercurrent in his personality. Alcohol had been known to affect the band's live performances, too. Concerts began well and sometimes went steadily downhill as he drank, until the night unraveled, like a spool of thread, into a messy tangle. Not long after I first interviewed Glen in Massachusetts, I drove to see Sticky Fingers perform at a little bar in rural Pennsylvania. When I mentioned it years later, Glen said, "Those shows escape me like my Capital One bills." I wasn't sure if he'd forgotten or was pretending to have forgotten, though, because only about fifteen people had shown up, and Glen had gotten drunk and nearly fallen off the stage.

The wild, incorrigible, substance-addled band member is a rock and roll cliché—but for them, who would trash hotel rooms and make lewd advances toward flight attendants? But rarely is that person the leader of the band—a circumstance of life in Sticky Fingers that tended to place the other musicians in compromising situations. A drummer named Paul Scali who occasionally played with Sticky Fingers told me one such story: "We were playing out in New Jersey at this concert on a military base," Scali said. "It was like a fair with kids' rides and stuff. Glen is absolutely pickled and he starts swearing over the microphone. All these military guys come up to the foot of the stage and one says, 'You shouldn't be swearing. I've got an eleven-year-old daughter.' These military guys are getting *pissed*! I'm looking at Angello, who was playing bass, and I'm like, 'Let's get out of here as soon as the show ends or we're going to get our asses kicked.' This goes on for a while. Finally, the soundman literally pulled the plug on Glen."

I once asked Glen about his drinking, and he allowed that there had been times when he'd drunk too much onstage but said it was usually a result of the day-to-day condition of being a rock and roll musician. "I'm not making any excuses," he said, "but most people who go to work show up with eight hours' sleep. When we arrive at work, it's after traveling all night to get there. You didn't sleep. You didn't eat. You sit around for another five hours, promoters are buying you drinks. These drinks just appear in your hand. Somebody hands you a cranberry and vodka, you drink it like it's cranberry." Glen paused a moment and seemed to consider the point. "I do have an open drinking and drug policy in the band," he said. "As long as you can do what you need to do. This is rock and roll. A couple of cocktails just tears down any wall as far as what you're doing. To go out there sober and sound stiff? That's not what the Stones fans want to see."

Despite the tumult, or because of it, or perhaps due to some blessed combination, Sticky Fingers has prospered under Glen's leadership. The band has been together in one form or another for almost thirty years—a lifetime in rock and roll, nearly as long as U2 and R.E.M. and longer than the Beatles remained together by almost two decades. Before Jon Bon Jovi sang with the band in Atlantic City, he turned to Hal Selzer and said, "Is this the same Sticky Fingers from when we were kids?" In fact, I was frequently amazed by the band's renown, especially in the Northeast where many older rock fans recalled seeing Sticky Fingers at one now-shuttered rock club or another, and by the way Glen, through impersonating a celebrity, had become somewhat of a celebrity in his own right. Everyone in the tribute world seemed to know him, and on several occasions his name came up in the most unlikely situations. Once, I was in a bar in Manhattan doing an interview, and when I happened to mention Sticky Fingers a guy walking past the table stopped and asked the person I was with, "Are you Glen Carroll?"

Of course, a large part of the band's success is due to the enormous popularity of the Stones, who, along with the Beatles, are the most influential band in rock history. The Stones have been together for more than forty years and have sold more than 200 million albums by some estimates. Played in endless rotation on classic rock radio, the band's songs have attained the deep-rooted familiarity of nursery rhymes. Sometimes at a Sticky Fingers concert, the band will do a set that includes "Start Me Up" and "Brown Sugar" and "Miss You" and "Honky Tonk Women" and "Sympathy for the Devil" and "Satisfaction"—and just when I think the band is running out of hits, I hear "Under My Thumb" and "Ruby Tuesday" and "Paint It, Black" and "Jumpin' Jack Flash," and a dozen more. It's a good time to be a Stones tribute band; the Internet has widened Glen's reach, and as the baby boomers age the music of their youth seems only to grow in popularity and commercial appeal. You can't turn a radio dial without hearing "Hotel California" or "Sweet Home Alabama" or a "get the led out" block of Led Zeppelin. Classic rock has become the sound track of the advertising industry, used to sell cars ("Go Your Own Way"), accounting firms ("Taxman"), tampons ("Time of the Season"), cell phones ("People Got to Be Free"), hamburgers ("You've Got Another Thing Coming"), blue jeans ("Back in

Black"), beer ("Simple Man"), lingerie ("Love Sick"), the U.S. Postal Service ("Fly Like an Eagle"), the presidency ("Don't Stop"), and so on.

A great number of people would like the Rolling Stones to play their birthday party, or wedding reception, or frat house, or Fourth of July barbecue but happen to be on a tight budget and don't happen to be acquainted with the Rolling Stones, so they hire Sticky Fingers. In recent years, the band has developed a mildly lucrative and fairly consistent routine: in the spring Sticky Fingers plays the southern fraternity circuit; summer is the season for town fairs and music festivals; in the fall, it's back to the frat houses. Mixed in are casino dates, corporate engagements, and the occasional far-flung booking in, say, Panama. Sticky Fingers commands between $2,500 to $5,000 per gig, which means that on a $3,500 engagement, after Glen has paid the other four members $250 a piece, then shelled out another $1,000 or more in expenses (gas, food, hotel), he walks away with around $1,500, which isn't bad compensation for singing "Satisfaction" and dancing around for a few hours. The band members still drive seventeen hours to perform but just as often now they fly, as they did not long ago when Sticky Fingers was hired to entertain the employees of Genentech, a biotech firm, at its annual Christmas party. The band was flown to the company headquarters in San Francisco, put up in the Hyatt, and given the rock-star treatment, despite a clause in the contract strictly forbidding "tight pants."

"It was the most professional show this band has done," Dan told me, happily stressing *professional*.

I asked him if his second time in Sticky Fingers had been better than the first.

"I have no problems at all with Glen now and don't think I ever will again," he said, then added, "Glen is a great guy. He's a dick, too, but he's a great guy."

One night a few weeks after the Hampden-Sydney show, Sticky Fingers played a gig closer to my home, at a bar in Queens called Cassidy's Tavern. It was a rarity on two accounts. Although the members of Sticky Fingers live in or near New York City, the band rarely performs in the city itself because venues there tend not to pay very well. And Glen avoids bars in general, adhering to what he calls his "Five C's Principle," which states that the most money to be made, under the best working conditions, is in playing corporate events. This is followed by casinos, colleges, carnivals or town fairs, and, lastly, clubs and bars. At a bar, the sound system is generally inferior, and if the turnout is low, the owner will sometimes try to cut a deal, rather than paying the band the agreed-upon fee.

Cassidy's was set amid a bustling strip of nightclubs and restaurants near the elevated subway tracks. When I arrived, Dan was on the bar's tiny stage, sitting behind a drum kit that appeared to be made of black rubber. He looked perplexed. "The stage is so small, they've got me playing electronic drums," he said.

He turned to the soundman and asked if the electronic drums would be sufficiently amplified. "Don't worry," the soundman said. "It'll sound like Madison Square Garden in here."

After a moment, Dan got up and walked to the dressing area, a storage closet in the back of the bar that had been furnished with a couple of bar stools, a wobbly table, and a refrigerator full of Budweiser for the band. In the room was Kevin

Gleeson, the band's new Keith, the one Dan and George had described to me as "the Keithiest" Keith they had ever seen. He was
already dressed in his stage outfit: a tank top with crescent-shaped
rips along the bottom that exposed his skinny abdomen and a pair
of vintage flare-legged jeans. But the masterstroke was his hair. It
was at once matted and frizzy, and appeared to contain within it
various trinkets: foreign coins, African jewelry, pieces of animal
bone. I later learned the items were actually attached to a leather
headband onto which he had glued clumps of his own hair. The
effect was rock and roll pirate.

Until I met Kevin Gleeson, I had assumed it was impossible
to re-create the withered visage of Keith Richards, who, through
a combination of drug abuse, lack of sleep, poor dentistry, and
decades spent living within a cloud of cigarette smoke, has ac-
quired a corpselike mien. But Kevin looked remarkably similar to
Richards, down to the wolfish features and spectacularly rotted
teeth. On road trips, I would come to learn, he mirrored
Richards's gypsy-like living habits, too; he ate little and slept less.
He once told me his only pieces of furniture were "guitars and
amplifiers." By his own account, Kevin is a recovering alcoholic
and a former heroin addict, which lent him an ultimate verisimilitude in the role. As it happened, the show at Cassidy's was a
homecoming of sorts. For the past decade, he had lived with his
wife and two sons in Chicago, but two months earlier, at the age
of forty-five, he had moved back to Queens, where he was raised,
in part to join Sticky Fingers, in part to take a job as a graphic
artist with the New York Police Department. Kevin is kind-
hearted, somewhat meek, consistently without funds, and believes
sincerely in the mythos of rock and roll. In his pants pockets he
carries dirt taken from the Mississippi Delta, birthplace of the

blues. That night, Kevin was wearing cowboy boots, and I asked him what they were made of.

"Snakeskin," he said in a fabulously scratchy Queens accent. "These boots are vintage '69 Keith Richards. Just like in the movie *Gimme Shelter* when he's recordin' 'Love in Vain' and tappin' his foot with the front of the boot blown out." I looked down at Kevin's feet; the fronts of the boots were authentically blown out.

All this time, Dan had been studying a typewritten set list of songs that Kevin had drawn up, per Glen's request, and his brow was furrowed. "This is crazy. This is just crazy," Dan said to Kevin. "I'm telling *you* before Glen gets here. 'Thru and Thru'—don't know it. It's going to go over like a lead balloon. 'The Nearness of You'—don't know it. Another lead balloon."

"The Stones played it all last tour," Kevin said. "It's by Hoagy Carmichael."

Dan shook his head. "This is a fucking mistake for this bar, tonight, in New York City," he said. " 'Salt of the Earth'—thank God, at least *there's* a song I know."

Kevin shrugged. "I'm like a hired gun. I do what I'm told."

"I hear you," Dan said. "Unfortunately, the way these songs are set is embarrassing for somebody like me. I have my friends coming tonight to see *a Stones show*. They're not going to care about this shit."

Just then, George Steckert breezed into the room, followed by Glen, who had flown in for the weekend from Winter Haven, Florida, where he recently moved into a house a few doors down from his parents. (He'd broken up with the girlfriend in New Jersey.)

"Oh! The whole motley crew is here," Glen said, suddenly lifting the mood. "How's Dangerous Dan?"

"You're a cocksucker," Dan said. He was always upset with Glen over one thing or another. "You gotta be kidding me with this set list."

"Tell me what's scaring you," Glen said.

"No one knows these songs," Dan said, in a whiny tone.

From across the room, Kevin said, "If you've seen the Stones recently, this is what they're doing."

Glen shrugged, as if the matter were out of his control. "This is what they're doing now, Dan," he said.

"I don't believe it. I just don't believe it," Dan said.

Glen seemed distracted. "Did anybody see that Puerto Rican hottie at the end of the bar?" he asked. Turning to Dan, who was holding a beer, he said, "Where did you find the cold beverages?"

The conversation turned to a press conference held by the Rolling Stones at Lincoln Center four days earlier to announce the band's upcoming tour. Perhaps owing to the Stones' advanced ages, the event had been fairly subdued compared to previous publicity stunts, which included performing "Brown Sugar" while driving down Fifth Avenue on a flatbed truck ('75) and landing in a Bronx park in a blimp ('02). The tour, ostensibly in support of a new studio album, *A Bigger Bang,* was scheduled to begin on August 21 in Boston and to include more than thirty-five U.S. dates, as well as a sweep through South America, the Far East, and Europe. A special stage set was being constructed so that a select number of fans could watch the show onstage with the Stones. "You'll get a great view of our bums," Mick Jagger had quipped to the assembled crowd of fans and reporters.

"The guy in the *Post* was ripping them, saying, 'Here come the granddads again,' " Dan said. "What, are you kidding me?"

"I heard that CC asked Mick a question at the press conference," George said, referring to the leader of Hot Rocks, a rival Rolling Stones tribute band from Philadelphia.

"He was brownnosing," Glen said. "He looked like a fucking chooch."

I asked Glen how the tour would affect Sticky Fingers.

"Like shaking a hornet's nest," he said, smiling wide. "I already got a call from a guy who runs the largest club in Boston. He wants me to play the three days up there before the Stones play. The Stones are back again, but they're still inaccessible. When they go on tour, radio stations run promotions"—here he affected a DJ's overheated delivery—" *'We're giving away five front-row tickets to the Rolling Stones. Come down to the Avalon! We have Sticky Fingers, the ultimate Stones tribute band!'* It creates a buzz."

As it happened, the band was trying out a new bass player that night, an acquaintance of Dan's named Alex Craven. (George had switched from bass to guitar to fill the vacant Ron Wood role.) Alex looked to be in his late thirties and had short brown hair and wore horn-rim glasses. He explained that he was on hiatus from his regular gig as the bassist for Bill Haley's Comets, an oldies act led by a drummer and former Comet named John "Bam Bam" Lane. The group performs at car shows out west and tours the Florida seniors circuit, competing for bookings with two other bands made up of former Comets: one named simply the Comets and a second one that also goes by the name Bill Haley's Comets but is led by a guy named Al Rappa. According to Alex, there was competitive bad blood between the bands. (Bill Haley, by the way, has been dead since 1981.)

"I got the gig because the longtime bass player has cancer of the leg," Alex said. "So far, it's been a real gas."

Glen changed into a pair of black stretch Lycra pants that Kevin had given him. "Kev, these pants are great," he said, eyeing himself in a mirror.

"Those pants, with the purple shirt—that's the Madison Square Garden show, last tour," Kevin said.

It was nearing 11:00 P.M. The bar was filled with people, many of them Rolling Stones fans, conspicuous in their Stones concert T-shirts. Glen gathered everyone in a team huddle. "Let's talk about these songs," he said, laying out his game plan. "I want the guitar players to communicate as to who's taking the solos. And I don't want to come out with 'Brown Sugar' and 'Start Me Up' right away, because what if people come late? You want to save the big hits. What I want to start doing is give these Rolling Stones and Sticky Fingers fans a real Keith fix. Kev, you can sing 'Thru and Thru' and 'The Nearness of You' without the band, right?"

Kevin nodded. Dan, George, and Alex stood at the dressing room door. The soundman cued up the band's intro tape, a symphonic version of "You Can't Always Get What You Want." As the tape played over the speakers and the crowd waited, Glen fussed with his hair. He'd recently had it cut and worried that it looked off. "The chick left the bangs long, no?" he said.

"No," Kevin said. "You're looking Mick. You're looking more Mick than I've ever seen."

3

Tribute bands are often called "cover bands," but the two are different by degrees: whereas a cover band plays a wide range of other artists' material, a tribute band dedicates itself wholly to the music of one particular group. The goal of a tribute band is to replicate as closely as possible, in both sound and appearance, another, more famous band. That way, fans of, say, the heavy-metal group Black Sabbath can see Sabbra Cadabra, "the world's greatest Black Sabbath tribute band," and hear their favorite music performed live. Tribute bands are in a sense a happy compromise: the musicians onstage would probably rather be *in* Black Sabbath and the audience would rather be *at* a Black Sabbath concert, but, in the absence of those options, Sabbra Cadabra is a fine substitute.

Tribute bands are a curious form of self-expression; the band members are basically pretending to be other people. They dress in costumes, mimic stage moves, learn songs note for note, affect an accent if required, use replica instruments, and alter their physical appearance with makeup or wigs. A few have gone further. Several years ago, a man named Dennis Wise quit his job as a used-car salesman and underwent surgery on his cheekbones, nose, lips, and mouth to look like Elvis Presley circa 1972. Wise was featured in a book about Elvis impersonators called *All the King's Men,* and in the book his manager, Colonel Jim Rowley, says, "Wouldn't you say that plastic surgery is the ultimate a person could do as a fan? It might be a form of fanaticism but Dennis Wise lives Elvis Presley. He eats it and sleeps it. If you were a girl on a date with Dennis you would end up watching a videotape of Elvis on tour." Wise's story is extreme, of course, but it illustrates what the writer Chuck Klosterman has called the "bizarre zero-sum game" all tribute bands are engaged in. "If a tribute band were to succeed completely," Klosterman observed, "its members would essentially cease to exist."

There are thousands of tribute bands, taking the world as a whole. Most pay homage to classic rock bands, but there are also tributes to country, soul, reggae, and blues artists. In fact, there are tributes to just about any band you would naturally think of and some you would never think of; a few years ago, a trumpet player in San Francisco formed a tribute to the easy-listening sounds of Herb Alpert and the Tijuana Brass. The most popular tend to re-create groups that can never be seen again in concert, like the Beatles, who have the most tributes to them—more than eighty—but there are also tributes to acts that tour regularly, like the Dave Matthews Band. Style, method, and degree of verisimilitude vary. The members of some tributes dress up and construct elaborate replica stage sets. Some don't bother with appearances at all but focus entirely on the music. Some pay tribute to a specific period of a band's career, like, say, Van Halen during the David Lee Roth years. Some are ironic, like Hair Supply, "the greatest heavy metal tribute to Air Supply in the Tri-State area!" Most are born out of fanlike devotion, and a few take a scholarly approach. Dark Star Orchestra replicates specific Grateful Dead concerts— say, Providence, Rhode Island, June 26, 1974.

A Web site called Tributecity.com is the Internet headquarters for tribute bands, offering articles of advice ("The Pitfalls of Your First Tribute Band"; "Combating the Big Gig Blues") and an extensive database of tributes around the globe. People are often astounded by the sheer number and variety of tribute bands that exist. Among them are Alice Unchained, Motley CruD, Zoso, Looks That Kill, Duran Duran Duran, Strawberry Fields, BlonDee, Almost Queen, Dixie Chicklets, Coldplayer, Red Hot Chili Bastards, Dreamboat Annie, the Vibe Remains the Same, Zoo Station Cleveland, Allison Road, Anything for Loaf, Atomic Punks and twenty-five other tributes to Van Halen—including Hot for Teacher, Fair Warning, Van Hagar, and Van Heinekin— Rattle & Hum, Malice Cooper, Hysteria, Ashbone U Wish, OzMosis (and also OZZMosis), the Boys from Beatlemania, Sabbath Bloody Sabbath, the aforementioned Sabbra Cadabra, Steelin' Dan, Petty Theft, Pretend Pretenders, We Are Not Queen, Alanis Moreorless, Kounterfeit Kinks, Fake No More, 4 Way Street, 1234, 1988, 2 You, Hammer of the Gods, Hotel California, Hotter than Hell U.K., Jovi, Kinda Kenny—the ultimate tribute to Kenny Rogers—Limpish Bizkit, and Maiden NY. And briefly working backward alphabetically, Ziggy Barlust, the Wholigans,

Violet Eclipse (an Italian tribute to Yngwie Malmsteen), Unfor-
gettable Fire, and Trez Hombrez, who presumably compete with
Zoo Zoo Mud, "Missouri's tribute to ZZ Top." Then there are
Frontiers, Hangar 18, Alcoholica, Time in a Bottle, Tooth and
Nail—A Tribute to DOKKEN, Guns 2 Roses, Paradise City,
three bands named Appetite for Destruction, two female AC/DC
tributes—AC/DShe and Helles Belles—an all-girl Led Zeppelin
band called Lez Zeppelin, the Australian Pink Floyd Show, Fleet-
foot Mike, Fleetwood Bac, Gentlemen Prefer Blondie, KISSNA-
TION, KISSTHIS, KISSTORY, KIST, Negative Creep, Rod
Stewart Review, Think Floyd, Changes in Latitudes, Amorica—a
tribute to the Black Crowes, who themselves are a tribute to the
Rolling Stones and the Faces—Sample Minds, ABBABABES,
Abbagirls, Spinal Pap, Cowboys from Hell, the Beached Boys,
Space Truckin', Cold Gin, Exodus, the Cureheads, Forever
Everly, Shania Twin (not to be confused with Twain's Twin), the
Bootleg Doors, Surely Bassey!, the Bastard Son of the Nuge, Ants
Marching, British Steel, Lee Alverson as Elton John, Radioheart,
Ghost in the Machine, Seattle, Sinatra Style, Locomotive Breath,
State of Quo, Byrds of a Feather, Stayin Alive, the Phil Collins
Tribute, Bootylicious, Desperado, Balls to the Wall—one of *four*
tributes to the German heavy-metal band Accept—Bridge of
Sighs, Just Priest, Captain Fantastic, Gabba Gabba Heys, Is This
Tom Jones, Come Together, Hatful of Hollow, Dream Police,
Ragged Glory, Combat Rock, Dylanesque, Mama Kin, Hendrix
Rockprophecy, Pretzel Logic, and Night of the Living Floyd.

There are not one but *two* KISS tribute bands peopled by
dwarves—Mini Kiss and Tiny Kiss, respectively.

In the mid-nineties, an independent filmmaker named Russ

Forster drove around the country filming a documentary about tribute bands. In many ways, Forster was the perfect person to document the tribute world. Drawing on a modest inheritance, he makes charmingly amateurish films that concern themselves with fringe subcultures; his previous documentary, *So Wrong They're Right,* was an in-depth examination of eight-track enthusiasts. Forster became fascinated by tribute bands after seeing an AC/DC and Black Sabbath tribute double bill at a Chicago park in 1996, an afternoon he fondly recalls as "the most amazing, bizarre, white-trashy experience I think I've ever had." Forster spent the next three years filming tribute bands in their natural habitat—B-list rock clubs like the Crocodile Cafe in Seattle and the Rock 'n' Roll Café, the Greenwich Village nightspot where Sticky Fingers held residence.

The resulting film, *Tributary,* released in 2001, features, among others, two Black Sabbath bands, the world's first Captain Beefheart tribute, a Guided by Voices act whose members all swear they would "take a bullet" for GBV founder Bob Pollard, and an illuminating interview with the members of Aces High—a KISS band made up entirely of Ace Frehleys. The film's grainy live footage and shaky camera work only underscore the earnest appeal of Forster's chosen subject. Tribute bands are a simulation, but at the same time they are affectingly genuine; the musicians aren't guided by commercial interests or a record company marketing strategy, but in most cases by a sincere desire to perform. And tribute bands are pretested entertainment: if you like the Rolling Stones, you will like Sticky Fingers. On the other hand, if you pay ten dollars to see an original-music act you've never heard before, it's a gamble; you might discover a favorite new artist or spend the night listening to a shrill woman with an acoustic guitar sing fourteen songs about her ex-boyfriend. Perhaps most importantly, tribute bands are accessible. Aerosmith is never going to play your local sports bar. Draw the Line, however, will come and sing "Walk This Way," and you won't have to spend a lot of money or wait an hour on the phone with Ticketmaster to see them. At the show, you can stand right in front, take pictures, dance with friends, meet the band, and interact with the music and musicians in a remarkably direct way. At one point during *Tributary,* at a performance by a Mötley Crüe band, a metalhead in the audience tells Forster, "I like these guys better than the real Mötley Crüe because they're playing the same music, but I'm closer, I'm there, you know. They care about *me.* They don't care about their albums and their record contract."

Not everyone is a fan of tribute bands, of course. Some view tribute bands with puzzlement, and a few see them as an affront to the very idea of rock and roll as unbridled creative expression. Why don't you play your own music? the criticism goes. In fact, many tribute musicians have played their own music and found the experience disheartening. "You'd drive a hundred miles and play for ten people," a guitarist named Lenny Mann told me. Mann is the founder of Tributecity.com, and before he became involved in the tribute world he spent the eighties in an original rock band called Island. At one point, the members of Island moved from Hollywood to Minneapolis when it was rumored that bands there were being signed to record deals. The relocation did not improve their prospects. When the group disbanded, Mann found himself playing Jimmy Page in a tribute to Led Zeppelin, called Led Zepplica. The band performed in front of five thousand people at a college festival in India and recently did a national tour of concert halls in Canada.

For his part, Russ Forster believes that tribute bands can be just as creative as bands that perform their own songs, and on this point he mentions the Brothers E—two generously proportioned guys from Portland, Oregon, who perform together as Elvis impersonators in matching white jumpsuits. "When I first heard about the concept, it sort of blew me away," Forster recalled. "It was a very creative way of doing something that had been done a million times before. I often ran into interesting pairings that created this whole what-if world. Like what if the Beatles played live with the Stones, and Paul McCartney sang a duet with Mick Jagger on 'Satisfaction'? In the tribute world, you can go places reality cannot possibly go."

By the end of *Tributary*, several truths about the tribute world emerge: 1) Singers in Black Sabbath bands never seem to resemble Ozzy Osbourne but somehow all look alike. 2) Tribute musicians take a strange pride in being authentically derivative (a KISS band that even buys makeup from the same company as KISS). 3) When talking about their craft, tribute musicians will inevitably commit what Forster calls "the ultimate tribute band faux pas" by claiming to play better than the band they're paying tribute to. 4) Nearly all tribute musicians believe modern rock pales in comparison to the classic rock of their 1960s and 1970s youth. "Everything that's good today is based on Sabbath," the singer of Sabbra Cadabra tells Forster outside of the Rock 'n' Roll Café. "Anything that's shitty is based on . . . well . . . I don't know . . . shit." When Forster asks another member of Sabbra Cadabra, a bearded guy in a motorcycle jacket, if the band has ever attempted to write its own songs, the man offers a "What's the point?" shrug and replies, "Yeah, we attempted it a coupla times—sounded just like Black Sabbath."

Like many things in popular music, the idea of tribute bands began with the Beatles, or, rather, with *Beatlemania,* a Broadway musical based on the Beatles. The show was the inspiration of a crafty music manager named Steve Leber, who one afternoon in 1976 was at home on Long Island and heard his daughter and her friends singing Beatles songs. Leber regarded the Beatles as his generation's answer to Beethoven, but was nevertheless surprised to hear a new crop of teens singing "Love Me Do." Since a Beatles reunion was unlikely, he decided to create a tribute—a Broadway musical that would celebrate his idols and, as he once said, "pay homage to the group's guiding influence during the turbulent sixties." Also, he figured he could make a lot of money.

At the time, Leber's business partner was David Krebs, and Leber-Krebs management represented some of the biggest names in rock, including Aerosmith, AC/DC, and Ted Nugent. Initially, Leber didn't tell his music-industry friends about his idea, and the few he did tell laughed and said, "Who wants to see four guys dressed as the Beatles?" For *Beatlemania* to succeed, Leber knew the group had to not only sound like the Beatles but, more important, *look* like them. He placed an ad in the *Village Voice* seeking Beatle look- and sound-alikes to audition for "a unique opportunity," and he hired Kenny Laguna, who had played in Tommy James and the Shondells and later worked on a lot of bubblegum hits like "Yummy Yummy," to hold auditions at S.I.R. studios in Manhattan. One day, a twenty-three-year-old guitarist from Long Island named Mitch Weissman walked into the studio. Weissman so resembled the young Paul that another person auditioning thought, Why is Paul McCartney here? Once Leber found his Paul, the rest of the cast fell into place around him. A guitarist from the Bronx, Joe Pecorino, was cast as John Lennon; Justin McNeill became Ringo Starr; and George Harrison was now a buck-toothed guy named Leslie Fradkin. Of the four, only Les Fradkin had any real music-industry experience. Under the name Fearless Fradkin, he had released a single, "Son of a Thousand Voices," b/w "You Can Cry If You Want To"; guested on a record by the avant-garde folk band the Godz; and formed the short-lived trio Thornton, Fradkin & Unger, which you could think of as a far less successful Crosby, Stills & Nash.

For close to a year, the four cast members rehearsed five days a week, several hours a day, at S.I.R. studios, analyzing the Beatles' career with the academic rigor of a scientist decoding a DNA strand. They scrupulously studied how John held his Rickenbacker guitar, or the way Paul bobbed his head during the "whooh-oohs" in "I Saw Her Standing There." Film projectors were set up to screen newsreels of old press conferences and the Beatles' first American concert, at Washington Coliseum in Washington, D.C. A language coach was brought in to teach the cast to speak with a Liverpudlian accent. Sometimes, Leber would invite music-industry bigwigs, like Dick Clark or Walter Yetnikoff, then president of CBS Records, to the rehearsals and lobby them to invest in the show (Yetnikoff became an early investor).

Even before he'd assembled a cast and secured funding, Leber had first investigated the legal issues surrounding *Beatlemania*. It was unclear whether he could stage a Broadway show featuring the music of the Beatles without being sued by the Beatles themselves. "The truth is, if I went to John and the band and said, 'I want to do a show about you called *Beatlemania*,' they would have thought I was out of my mind," Leber, who has since retired from band management but is still involved in the music business, told me when I visited him one afternoon in his office on lower Broadway in Manhattan. "The Beatles didn't understand how much the public really wanted to see them." Leber is a robust man in his early sixties and has a gregarious and pleasantly self-satisfied manner; we spoke in a conference area that doubled as a sort of trophy room for his career, the walls decorated with gold and platinum records awarded to the bands he managed. According to Leber, he did approach Paul McCartney's attorney, John Eastman, who told him the Beatles weren't likely to be receptive. Instead, he contacted the company that managed the publishing for the Beatles song catalog and secured the "grand rights"—that is, the rights to use the songs in a theatrical setting. Under the arrangement, he could use the group's material so long as he paid royalties to the publishing company, who, in turn, would pay the Beatles. Leber still felt he was in murky territory legally, so he hired two separate law firms specializing in copyright law to draft an opinion stating that he could produce a Broadway show based on the Beatles without the group's consent. He also instructed the cast members never to introduce one another onstage by their Beatle names but, rather, as "my friend." Finally, under advisement from his lawyers, he slapped the disclaimer "Not the Beatles but an incredible simulation" onto everything associated with the production: playbills, posters, newspaper ads, the ends of TV and radio spots.

There was, of course, still the matter of creating a Broadway show. There really wasn't anything theatrical about playing Beatles songs in front of an audience. Leber hired the noted lighting designer Jules Fisher and Lynda Obst, now a movie producer but then a magazine editor, to enliven the visual elements. They came up with the idea of using the history of the sixties as a way to frame the music, so that images of the Kennedy assassination or civil rights marches and Vietnam protests were projected onto large screens while the cast played the most beloved sound track in music. The show was divided into two parts: the early "live" Beatles, with their mop-top hairdos and trim Chesterfield suits representing early sixties innocence, and the Sgt. Pepper–era "studio" Beatles. Many had never seen the Beatles in concert, and those who had seen the group perform live had never heard songs like "Strawberry Fields Forever," because the band had stopped touring in 1966. The show gave people a second chance to see the most influential band in the history of rock music.

Beatlemania made its debut at the Winter Garden Theatre on May 26, 1977. Today, Broadway is overrun with nostalgic productions built around a well-known catalogue of hits, like ABBA's *Mamma Mia!* or *Movin' Out,* which pairs the songs of Billy Joel with interpretive dance. But *Beatlemania* didn't resemble anything that had come before: there was no real "book," or story, and very little dialogue; the only original element was the concept. Without the visual distractions, it was basically a Beatles concert performed by four guys who weren't the Beatles. Leber knew the critics would hate it. So as a countermove, he focused on attracting audiences unlikely to be swayed by reviews, like suburban teenagers and families, and also created one of the first television ad campaigns using audience testimonials. In the commercials, a member of the audience would exit the theater, look at the camera, and say something enthusiastic, like, "They look and sound just like the Beatles. You won't believe it!" As a final precaution, he never officially opened the show. Instead, he stayed in previews because critics usually waited until after opening night to publish a review. By the time the critics figured out what he was doing, it was too late: *Beatlemania* was a smash hit.

For a while, the cast members were content to set aside their own musical ambitions and enjoy the spoils of being stars on Broadway. There were profiles in *People, Newsweek,* and *Rolling Stone,* and TV and radio appearances. "I was making, like, fifteen hundred dollars a week and driving a Mercedes-Benz," Mitch Weissman told me. "My rent was only two hundred and seventy-five dollars a month, so how much money did I need?" Weissman was the show's lead—the face. Reviews cited his "uncanny" portrayal of Paul McCartney and he appeared on the TV show *Kids Are People, Too* to sing "Yesterday." Rumors circulated that the Beatles were angry and planned to bring a lawsuit, and that the production would be shut down. But the production wasn't shut down. The theater kept filling each night. (*Beatlemania* eventually grossed over forty million dollars.) Leber envisioned a *Beatlemania* empire, with productions around the world and "bus and truck" companies touring the country.

In January 1978, the cast flew to Los Angeles to open *Beatlemania* at the Shubert Theatre in Century City, which necessitated assembling two more bands: one to understudy the new Broadway cast (the old understudies) and a second to understudy the original cast, now in California. In short, each new *Beatlemania* production required assembling two more groups. The task of finding, rehearsing, and managing the growing brood of fake

Beatles fell to Sandy Yaguda, a former member of Jay and the Americans, who was hired as musical director. "It was like *American Idol* for the Beatles," Yaguda told me. "You would sit in this audition room and go through a thousand people and maybe find four who were good enough." (At one casting call in Los Angeles, a man auditioning for the role of Paul McCartney was Vietnamese.) When a new crop of fake Beatles were rounded up, they were sent to S.I.R. studios for finishing school. To keep everyone straight, Yaguda, in the role of camp counselor, referred to the various groups as "Bunks"—as in Bunk One, Bunk Two, Bunk Three, eventually going all the way up to Bunk Ten. As the bunk numbers rose, the overall quality of musicianship and resemblance to any given Beatle tended to decrease; one of the later Ringos was hired mainly because he'd been a starting center fielder for the University of Miami and could anchor *Beatlemania*'s Broadway softball team. Moreover, the musicians were all young and ambitious and there were constant disputes and grievances—the Paul in Bunk Six felt he deserved to be in Bunk Three, say—which Yaguda had to sort out. "I was like the principal in a high school of Beatles," he said.

As the production wore on, the original cast members became restless in their narrow roles and tired of the nightly suppression of self required to be a fake Beatle. "You have to realize that at that point, I'd done five or six hundred shows or some crap like that," Les Fradkin told me. "It's, like, how much more do I have to do, please?" The cast members all hoped to use *Beatlemania* as a springboard to launch their own careers, and there was talk in the Leber-Krebs offices of recording an album as an original band, but it never materialized. For Leber, turning the cast members into artists independent from the show would have been self-defeating; he needed them to open new productions. Eventually, *Beatlemania* ran its course, and in the fall of 1979 the show ended its Broadway run. The show continued to tour small cities into the mid-eighties, and in 1981 Leber produced a film version of *Beatlemania.* But the movie flopped, and it turned out to be the fatal misstep in Leber's legal tightrope walk. The surviving Beatles eventually sued successfully on the grounds of right of privacy. All productions of *Beatlemania* were shut down. The court ruling further barred Leber from ever using the *Beatlemania* name again—a decision that haunts him to this day, considering a revival would no doubt earn him millions in box office receipts.

One night in 1996, soon after Russ Forster began filming his documentary *Tributary,* he went to a concert by the southern rock band Molly Hatchet. The band had been hugely popular in the late seventies and early eighties with the kinds of rock fans who respond to three "lead" guitarists and Frank Frazetta album-cover paintings of ax-wielding Vikings. But at the point Forster saw the band, Molly Hatchet was in a long commercial decline and attempting a comeback. The posters said MOLLY HATCHET, but it seemed like a liberal description; not one musician onstage had been an original member of the group, and the singer was formerly in a Southern rock cover band. Forster was genuinely unsure if he was seeing Molly Hatchet or a Molly Hatchet tribute band. "It really could have been either," he said, still sounding confused years later. "It could have been Molly Hatchet in a state of great decay or a tribute band getting pretty tight."

The line between tribute bands and the bands they pay tribute to has become increasingly blurred in recent years. On any night of the week, in any part of the country, you can find a tribute band performing—often at the same venues where famous bands play. Lez Zeppelin, an all-girl Led Zeppelin band, has sold out the Bowery Ballroom in Manhattan. In the sixties, the Doors were the house band at the Whisky A Go-Go on the Sunset Strip in Los Angeles; today, on a Saturday night at the Whisky you can see Wild Child, a Doors tribute. It's not uncommon for a tribute band to play a venue one week and, say, DOKKEN to play there the next. As tribute bands climb the music ranks and once-popular bands fall out of fashion, the two seem to meet in the middle—the middle being the state fair/Indian casino/local rock club circuit. Concert promoters, wanting to satisfy audiences, routinely hire tribute bands for outdoor rock festivals, rounding out a bill that might include Steppenwolf and .38 Special with a band like Sticky Fingers—which over the years has shared the stage with a cut-out bin of classic rockers, among them Eddie Money, April Wine, Rick Derringer, Pat Benatar, Dr. Hook, Foreigner, Big Brother and the Holding Company, Edgar Winter, and the Spencer Davis Group. In some cases, a popular tribute band can earn more than a band signed to a record label. Badfish, a tribute to the Southern California reggae-ska band Sublime, played 152 dates in 2006, selling 99,896 tickets and grossing $1.4 million.

Of the many tribute bands formed to entertain themselves and local audiences, a small number, perhaps two dozen, have become professional—that is, they are represented by managers and booking agents, tour nationally, sell merchandise, and earn a full-time living. In short, they seem like any other successful group in every way but the most obvious: they are pretending to be someone else. Sticky Fingers belongs in this category, as do Badfish; the Neil Diamond tribute Super Diamond; Dark Star Orchestra; the Aerosmith band Draw the Line; the Beatles acts 1964 and Rain; and the Led Zeppelin tribute Zoso. Wherever I went, I was told how good Zoso were and that I had to see them in concert. A Princeton graduate told me the band was so popular at the university that the eating clubs compete to book them for parties. Then she bestowed upon Zoso the highest compliment that can be paid to a tribute band: *"They sound just like Led Zeppelin!"*

I did see Zoso perform, at the Three Little Bakers Dinner Theatre in Wilmington, Delaware, and it stands as one of the best tribute shows I've seen, despite the very un–rock and roll setting, which included a brief performance by an elderly vaudeville acrobat, one of the three little bakers of name. Each time I closed my eyes, I was transported to Madison Square Garden circa 1975. I could almost see the facial hair and smell the pot smoke—an illusion broken only by the clanging of silverware on dinner plates. Like the best tribute performers, the members of Zoso are not only good mimics but also excellent musicians with the charisma and talent to have been actual rock stars had they caught a few lucky breaks. I had talked on the phone a few weeks earlier with the band's singer, Matt Jernigan, who told me he'd spent two decades singing in original bands (including an early version of Pantera) and scuffling around the edges of the music business before finding success with Zoso in 1995. At that time, Jernigan, who grew up in the South, was living in Hollywood—one of a generation of musicians raised on seventies hard rock only to find themselves out of favor with record executives when grunge and indie rock became popular. Jernigan is tall and rangy and has a mane of curly blond hair, like Robert Plant. A manager suggested he do a tribute to Led Zeppelin. "He goes, 'Man, you got a stompin' band, dude. It'd be a shame to see you guys not play together or do something substantial,' " Jernigan recalled. "We started doing shows and, man, it just took off. We took a three-week break in ninety-seven, and ever since then we've been hitting it hard." Zoso plays about 150 concerts a year—at bars, rock clubs, outdoor festivals, and what Jernigan, in his mellow southern accent, calls "thee-ate-ers." To keep pace with the bookings, the band tours with two matching sets of equipment, a concept Jernigan lifted from Pink Floyd. Jernigan said, "Floyd's show was so massive, they couldn't tour any other way, so I thought, Well, man, why can't we do that on our level? When I bought my first box truck, a Penske van, I didn't sell it, and I bought another one two years later. I said to the guys, 'Look, this is what we need to do—everybody needs to double up on their gear. Why? Well, because it's an investment and because we're losing important shows we could be doing.' So this means our bass player has two Ampeg rigs. He's got *six* Fender jazz basses. Our guitar player has *two* double-neck guitars, four Les Pauls, three Danelectros, two acoustics. Our keyboard player has double keys, and we have two drum kits. See, we have spec gear. Where on the road are you gonna find a coupla one-hundred-watt plexis? Where are you gonna find a twenty-six-inch amber drum kit? You aren't. So we'll tell our roadie, 'Okay, man, we need you to take one of the trucks and drive ahead of time to whatever town we're playing and secure it with the club owner.' We fly in and do the gig, with our gear already there. Then we'll fly to another gig somewhere else, with the *other* gear waiting on us."

While tribute bands like Zoso are becoming more professional, many famous older groups, depleted of both original members and hit records, have started to appear like glorified tributes to their former selves. When Queen singer Freddie Mercury died, in 1991, many people naturally assumed it marked the end of Queen. How could the band continue without its leader and without one of the most peerless singers in rock? In 2005, the remaining members did just that when they re-formed to tour with Paul Rodgers of Bad Company. (Paradoxically, when the Queen tribute Sheer Heart Attack lost its Freddie Mercury, the band dissolved.) Among others, the Cars, the Doors, Journey, INXS, Thin Lizzy, and Lynyrd Skynyrd have toured in recent years without their original lead singer. In the case of Lynyrd Skynyrd, whose career has the aspect of a Greek tragedy, vocalist Ronnie Van Zant died in 1977, when the band's plane crashed in rural Mississippi; a drunk-driving accident paralyzed lead guitarist Allen Collins in 1986 (he later died of pneumonia); and bassist Leon Wilkeson died in 2001. Strictly speaking, is seeing three-sevenths of the classic Lynyrd Skynyrd lineup all that different from seeing a really smoking Lynyrd Skynyrd tribute band? Taking this question to its logical conclusion, the manager of KISS has suggested replacing the aging members with younger musicians so the band can be franchised. "KISS is more like Doritos or Pepsi, as far as a brand name is concerned," he told a reporter.

Some tribute bands have performed with the acts to which they are paying tribute—as when Battery opened for Metallica on the Garage Inc. tour, or when Neil Diamond dueted with Surreal Neil, his counterpart in Super Diamond. And a few musicians have assumed the role they portray. The most famous case of this is Tim Owens, an office-supply salesman from Akron, Ohio, who in the mid-nineties went from singing in a Judas Priest tribute band called British Steel to actually singing in Judas Priest. (His story inspired the movie *Rock Star.*) As a teenager, Owens was uncommonly devoted to Judas Priest; he covered his bedroom walls with Priest posters, and on his eighteenth birthday he ate a cake decorated with a frosted image of the horned creature from the *Defenders of The Faith* album cover. Adult life followed along similar lines. Owens sold office supplies part-time and on weekends toured East Coast factory towns with British Steel. Around this time, Judas Priest was searching for a new singer because their old one, Rob Halford, had quit the band and announced that he was gay—a revelation that shocked the heavy-metal world but one that, in retrospect, was not surprising, given Halford's flair for prancing around onstage in studded leather outfits. Halford has one of the most distinctive voices in rock, a kind of operatic high wail, and finding a replacement proved difficult. According to a *New York Times* article about Owens, "a remarkable series of chance events" brought him to the band's attention. Actually, two acquaintances of the band, a tanning-parlor attendant from western New York named Christa Lentine, and her cousin, Julie Vitto, passed along a grainy video of Owens performing with British Steel at a club in Erie, Pennsylvania, called Sherlock's. In high school, Owens had sung in a madrigal choir, which strengthened his vocal cords, and he'd perfected his stage moves in the tribute band, so he looked and sounded remarkably like Rob Halford. "We'd listened to literally thousands of singers," Glenn

Tipton, Judas Priest's guitarist, told the *Times*. "Russian Eskimos, men, women, people from all corners of the world, knowns, unknowns. But here we knew without a shadow of a doubt we'd found our man." Tim Owens, paper-supply salesman from Akron, flew to Wales to audition and came back as "Ripper" Owens. Owens spent seven years in Judas Priest (Rob Halford eventually returned) and became a folk hero in the tribute world.

During the subsequent years, a reverse trend has taken place, as a number of musicians recognized on their own merits have formed tribute bands. Will Lee, the bassist in David Letterman's *Late Show* band, is also the slightly obsessive leader of the Fab Faux—a group of accomplished sidemen who re-create the music of the Beatles down to the last harmonium line. Lee told me he had reservations about forming the Fab Faux because he always thought tribute bands were hokey. "Just the very mention of what we are, a tribute band, is a turnoff," he said. "I don't understand the desire for grown men to pretend to be the Beatles, other than the financial aspect. I've seen the real Beatles, and I know you're not the real Beatles, so why are you creeping me out?" In the end, though, Lee, a lifelong Beatles fanatic, said he needed to form the band "for my soul."

Mike Portnoy, drummer for the progressive metal band Dream Theater, has formed four tribute bands—to the Beatles, to Led Zeppelin, to Rush, and to The Who. The bands are usually made up of Portnoy's friends, like singer Gary Cherone and the metal guitarist virtuoso Paul Gilbert, and play a short stand in big cities like New York and Los Angeles. It seems odd to form a tribute band *after* becoming a rock star; after all, someone in Progeny, a Dream Theater tribute band, is pretending to be Portnoy. But Portnoy told me, "It doesn't matter how many awards I win or how many millions of albums Dream Theater sells. I'm always going to look at myself as the kid on the other side of the stage. I'm still that Who/Zeppelin fan I was when I was twelve." In other words, being in a tribute band offers wish fulfillment even for musicians whose wishes have already been fulfilled.

4

Sticky Fingers isn't the only Rolling Stones tribute band. There is Hot Rocks, from Philadelphia. Also, the Rolling Clones, It's Only Rock 'n' Roll, Jumping Jack Flash, Midnight Ramblers, Shattered, the Counterfeit Stones (from Britain), and Satisfaction, among others. Sticky Fingers isn't even the only Sticky Fingers; a band in Southern California until recently went by the same name and people sometimes book that band, thinking they are hiring Glen Carroll's Sticky Fingers, and vice versa. The other Sticky Fingers recently changed their name to The Hollywood Stones to avoid confusion, but a kind of cat-and-mouse antagonism has developed between Glen and the rival band. At one point, I began to notice several shows listed on the "Tour Dates" section of the Sticky Fingers Web site that I had no recollection of the band playing, many of them in Southern California, including one at the Playboy Mansion. Dan eventually told me that not all the dates were real; Glen had invented some of them to rankle the guys in the other Sticky Fingers.

The most famous Stones tribute band—and Glen's main competitor—is the Blushing Brides, who bill themselves as "The World's Most Dangerous Tribute to the Music of the Rolling Stones" and have been around even longer than Sticky Fingers. The band formed in Kingston, Ontario, in 1978, and during the 1980s toured all over eastern Canada and the northeastern United States. The band's singer was a good-looking, muscular guy named Maurice Raymond, who had a dynamic stage presence and the self-possession of someone who knows he's going to be famous. Onstage, he hung from the rafters, flung his hair wildly, danced on tables, dowsed his naked chest with buckets of water. People waited in lines that stretched for blocks to see them. The Brides attracted the attention of RCA records and in 1982 released an album of their own songs. They did a tour of Canadian hockey arenas and had a single on the radio, but, oddly, the group soon went back to being a tribute band and spent the next several years playing Stones songs in bars and rock clubs.

By the time I became aware of the Brides, the original, key members were gone, but Maurice Raymond was still performing around New England with a new version of the band. I called the number on the Brides' Web site one day and ended up speaking to Kerry Muldoon—the same woman who arranged my first interview with Glen. Kerry explained that she had quit as the manager of Sticky Fingers a few years earlier, after a falling-out with Glen, and was now managing the Brides. Her boyfriend, Daniel Hoffenberg, had also quit Sticky Fingers and was now the Keith in the Brides. Kerry said working with Glen had been a "nightmare," although she didn't go into specifics, sounding as if she had experienced a horrible trauma and didn't want to relive it. It didn't matter anyway, she said, because the Blushing Brides were the greatest Stones band. "You're going to love Moe and the Brides," she said in a boosterish tone. "They really know how to play the Stones. Not like *Glen Carroll*!"

One Saturday in June, the Brides were scheduled to perform at the Trump Marina Hotel Casino in Atlantic City and I arranged to ride along. It wasn't the first time I'd met the band: a month earlier, the Brides had played at a bar in Rhode Island and I'd driven up from Brooklyn to see them. But I got caught in traffic and arrived late, and I only managed to see part of the show and speak briefly to Maurice and the other members backstage. The one thing I did take away from the meeting was that the Brides were a tribute band and not a "clone band," as Maurice termed it disdainfully. "We don't dress up like the Rolling Stones, and we don't play the songs note for note like these other clones," he said in a huff. "We play Rolling Stones music and put *our own* stamp on it!"

For the Atlantic City show, Maurice had flown from Calgary, where he lives, to join the rest of the band, who all reside in or near New York City. On Friday night, the Brides played the Cutting Room in Manhattan, and when I arrived at the drummer's apartment on Saturday morning to ride to Atlantic City, everyone was groggy from having been up late. Kerry Muldoon had rented a van for the band (she and Daniel Hoffenberg were driving separately, as was another guitarist, Lee Boice). Sitting inside was Rodney Ledbetter, the drummer; Larry Love, the bassist; and Shane McConnell, a former Bride who was sitting in with the group that weekend on guitar.

Maurice was in the driver's seat. He has fluffy brown hair, a prominent mouth, big white teeth, and a formidable upper body that rises from his waist like a V. He looks like Mick Jagger if Mick Jagger had spent a lot of time lifting weights. He has a similarly forceful conversation style, and soon after I climbed in the van, he was giving me a history lesson on Stones tribute bands. "The first fucking Stones band, *ever,* was in Canada," he said as we drove out of the city. "Hot Roxx—out of Toronto. Actually, there was another one out of Montreal called Silk n' Steel. And those cats were *fucking killer!* The guitar player's name was Merv or something. He's still around. But he's bulbous. Like this little guy that blew up into a bowling ball. I went to see them in seventy-three or seventy-four, when I was fourteen, in a little park in Montreal. They played like the Brides do—they played the shit nasty, like Stones music should be played. Of course, there was no Internet back then, so you didn't know who was doing what in California. Anyway, when we started, there was a band called Liverpool doing Beatles shit. In the States there was a Doors band called Crystal Ship. We wanted to play Stones but we wanted to do originals and become an original band that was like the *next* Stones. That's why we didn't call ourselves Sticky Fingers or Hot Rocks or whatever."

I asked him where the name Blushing Brides came from.

"Our manager," he said. "It has absolutely no connotations to the Stones."

"They just liked to wear dresses," Shane McConnell chimed in from the passenger seat. Shane is also Canadian and grew up in Sault Ste. Marie, or "the Soo"—as he calls it. He lived in Manhattan but for many years was a working musician in Toronto, where he'd met Maurice and the other guys in the original

Brides. He is tall and rangy, and has the same sly, offbeat handsomeness as the actor Jeff Goldblum, whom he loosely resembles. In style and manner, he appears less like a rock musician than a fifties-era hipster; that day, he wore black-frame glasses and a porkpie hat.

Maurice continued: "We played everything from juke joints to small arenas to soft-seat theaters. In the eighties, when there was still a good rock scene, we were on the B circuit. The A circuit was the big arenas. Like, when Joe Perry had the Joe Perry Project going on, we'd play the same-level rooms he did. It wasn't like we were doing Joe's Chicken Deli, although we did do some of those shitholes, because when you're doing five or six nights a week and six-week tours, you've got to do some shitholes."

In fact, Maurice, who grew up in Montreal, has been singing Stones songs his entire adult life. At fourteen, he joined a cover band called Jade, which performed material by groups like the Stones and the J. Geils Band. One night, in 1978, a guitarist named Paul Martin saw Jade perform at a little club in Montreal and approached Maurice after the show. As Maurice tells the story, the meeting carries the same weighted destiny as the one on a London train between the teenage Mick and Keith. Paul Martin was a fluid player, the kind who seems to have been born with a guitar in his hands. Also, he was a Stones fanatic. "Paul's the kind of guy," Shane said, "where somebody would go, 'I've got a bootleg that I don't think anyone has heard,' and Paul would go, 'Australia. Sunday afternoon, 1972. Keith was stoned on acid.' " Paul Martin was from Kingston, Ontario, and he asked Maurice to move there to start a band. The Blushing Brides, as they were named, were Maurice and Paul, along with two of Paul's friends from Kingston—Martin Van Dijk on bass and Richard "Ricco" Berthiaume on drums—and a guitarist from Montreal named James Green.

The Brides did Stones songs, but they put their own stamp on the music, playing a tighter, punchier, more aggressive version based on a Stones bootleg tape recorded on the band's '73 European tour. Known variously as *Bedspring Symphony* or *A Box Lunch and Meat Whistle,* the tape captures the Stones during an especially savage performance. With its buzz-saw guitars and heavy distortion, the version of "Doo Doo Doo Doo Doo (Heartbreaker)" on the album sounds like punk rock. The Brides used *Bedspring Symphony* as a template and then played a supercharged version of *that.*

The Brides were a sensational live band, and for three years they toured tirelessly on both sides of the border. The Brides played the El Mocambo in Toronto. They played the Shaboo Inn in Willimantic, Connecticut, and the Agora Ballroom in West Hartford. They played the Chaudière Rose Room, a big 4,500-seater up in Quebec, and the Misty Moon in Halifax, and Barrymore's Music Hall in Ottawa. Whenever they played the Channel in Boston, the line to get in stretched for a block. The Brides once performed at an amusement park in Rhode Island called Rocky Point, and so many people showed up—twenty thousand according to some versions of the story—that traffic clogged for miles and the band needed a police escort. At the time, the legal drinking age in many states was eighteen, and bars and clubs were so crowded with people wanting to party and hear live music that musicians were able to make a living even without a record deal. Sometimes, the Brides grossed eight thousand dollars a night. Often, the money was used to make their live show more dazzling:

the band had a thirty-two-channel Midas soundboard they bought from the guys in Supertramp, a light show, eight eighteen-inch speakers (four on each side of the stage), and pyrotechnics effects like concussion pots, which create a pressurized *BOOM!* "I literally saw people pass out from the shock of the concussion pots," Maurice said. "We used to tell people at gigs, 'Fifty of you will not make it past the first song.' " By 1980, the Brides were attracting so much attention that a *Boston Globe* reporter asked Mick Jagger what he thought of them, and whether he was bothered by their popularity. "No," Jagger replied in his characteristically cool way, "it's not offensive to me; it's just mad. . . . What can you do? What would Elvis have done? There are a lot of Elvis imitators, right? And then there's the *Beatlemania* thing, which did very well. I mean, the appetite for recycled crap in this country seems enormous."

When Maurice got to the part of the story that involved the band's debut album, *Unveiled,* and first national tour, he became less expansive. According to Maurice, the band members had been given a record deal largely on the strength of the live show and what few songs they had written were "infantile." The tour, opening for a Canadian rock band called Chilliwack, was "a disaster" and like starting again at the bottom. "For me, trying to present the songs as the front man, it was very frustrating to go from up here"—he lifted one hand off the wheel and held it high in the air—"to down here." It seemed an odd way to characterize the moment musicians work their entire life for: an album had been released by a major recording label, a song was on the radio, a big tour was lined up to bring the band to a larger audience. For the Brides on the cusp of success, to go back to being a tribute band was what seemed like starting over again. How had it happened? "The record company shot the dream out," Maurice said vaguely. "And then the band broke up. By the end of the tour, we were done."

A year or so after the tour, most of the members reunited, new guys were brought in, and the band stayed on the road for the next six years. In the mid-eighties, Mick Jagger and Keith Richards were feuding and the Stones had stopped touring altogether; rumors swirled that the Stones had broken up, and for fans the Brides became a substitute. They played between 150 and 200 concerts a year and toured in a customized van nicknamed "Blue Slumber." A five-man road crew and two trailers of gear followed behind. Lineup changes inevitably took place, but the Brides attracted top-notch replacements. "The thing about the Brides," Shane said, "is that because they made good money, it wasn't just a bunch of barroom players who were into the Stones. It was all these hot musicians. The Brides were one of the best bands in Canada, but they were a cover band. It was weird."

Then, in 1990, Paul Martin quit. According to Maurice, Paul had always wanted the Brides to grow beyond their most formative influence and he finally had enough of playing Stones music; he sold his collection of Stones memorabilia, renounced the tribute world, and struck out to do his own music. "Paul is troubled by this whole Stones thing in our past—it's something that weighs heavily on his conscience," Maurice said. "I mean, this is our life. We spent decades doing this." Maurice continued with other musicians for seven more years, but when the bookings began to dry up, he moved in 1997 with his wife and two sons to Calgary, where the economy was booming, and took his first day job. He continued to perform part-time with the Brides in both Canada and the States, and formed an American version of the band to cut out the travel costs of using Canadian musicians. That was the band I was seeing that weekend in Atlantic City.

Sitting in traffic on the Garden State Parkway, I asked Maurice if he was enthusiastic about the upcoming Stones tour. He shrugged. "I saw them in seventy-five and it was biblical, the last great Stones tour. Then I went in seventy-eight. I hitchhiked to Buffalo. It was horrible. For that kind of music, the scale was just too big. It loses something in the translation. Let's face it—seventy-five was their peak. Now it's a caricature. It's just a bunch of old songs that they package differently. People are hoping for some magic again, which is why they go see these clone bands."

I asked if the tour would at least bring him more work.

"In the early years, it was a good thing because it would boost up anything Stones-related," he said. "Now there are so many tribute bands. You look on the Web and there's a Sticky Fingers West, there's a Sticky Fingers East, there's a Hot Rocks Central. There's nothing special anymore." Once alone atop the tribute field, the Blushing Brides now competed for bookings with a dozen or more Stones bands, especially Sticky Fingers, who were equally well established on the East Coast. Just thinking about it infuriated Maurice. "These no-talent fucks like Glen fucking Carroll—*who I would strangle with my bare hands!*" he said, suddenly. "He's not a professional! He's not talented. None of these fuckers are. I hate to slag them, but you know what? Do something you're capable of. I'm capable of doing this. You're not. Fuck off!" The other band members sat in uncomfortable silence, as if waiting out a brief and violent storm. Maurice pressed

his point. "When he gets up there drunk and acts like an imbe-
cile," he said, referring to Glen, "it screws up my livelihood because then promoters go, 'We don't want to touch anything like
that anymore.' " Apparently, Sticky Fingers had been hired to play
the Trump Marina gig in past years, but the promoter had been
dissatisfied and this year hired the Brides.

Maurice looked in the rearview mirror and fixed his gaze to
the back of the van, where Larry Love, the bassist, was sitting.
Like Daniel Hoffenberg, Larry was a former member of Sticky
Fingers who had been recruited by Kerry Muldoon to play for
the Brides. He had long black hair, tanned skin the color of
caramel, and a fondness for wearing bandannas; he looked like
someone you might see walking the Sunset Strip in 1986. "Larry,
weren't you at this Trump gig and Glen was drunk or something?" Maurice asked.

"I've been at many gigs where Glen was drunk or something," Larry said, laughing. "Glen could be a pain in the ass, but
there are times I miss playing with him, bro. He would have me
laughing so hard, I'd be crying."

"Fucking Glen Carroll," Maurice said.

As we inched along in shore traffic, Maurice and Shane began to talk about former band members ("Anyone see Jack 'JackeeBoy' Fuller lately?"), and toss around old SCTV skits. A
number of stories involved buying or smoking hashish, which apparently was bountiful north of the border. "Do you remember
Al?" Maurice said.

"You mean Al the crazy Moroccan Jew?" Shane said.

Maurice turned to include the rest of us in the story. "This
guy was *nuts*. Remember I bought all that hash off him? He drove
up to Montreal with a big bag of it. I'm going, 'You drove with

that all the way from Toronto?' He had it, like, in the seat next to him, just sitting there. It was the biggest amount of hash I'd ever seen."

Shane said, "He once drove down the sidewalk on Spadina"—a busy street in downtown Toronto—"going thirty miles an hour in a Corvette." He was silent for a moment, then said, "We auditioned bass players one time for this band I was in and this one guy showed up every day with hash oil. At the end of the auditions, we all just looked at each other and went, 'Hash oil guy.'" Everyone laughed. "He brought hash oil to every gig," Shane continued, "and then one day he shows up with nothing. We're like, 'What do you mean you've got nothing? How do you think you got this gig? Get some fucking hash oil!'"

"Many cats got gigs like that—by being the drug guy," Maurice said knowingly. He looked impatiently at the sea of cars in front of us. "Where are all these people headed?" he said.

Just then, Shane looked out the window at a car in the neighboring lane. He seemed reminded of something. Then he said, "One time we were driving back from a gig, nice sunny day. I'm in the backseat. Moe says to me, 'Shane, you gotta look at these girls in the next car. They're stickin' their tongues out at us.' So I look over, and this old fat lady is driving and these two little girls are making these sexual gestures at us. These girls are, like, thirteen, just kids. All of a sudden, the fat lady pulls up beside us, lifts up her shirt, pulls her bra down, and shows us this gargantuan, massive whale tit. We're all going, *'Did ya fucking see that? Did ya?'*"

Maurice laughed at the memory and his mood lifted. "That became known as the Tit Episode in Brides lore," he said, laughing again.

"Ah, the rock and roll stories," Larry Love said from the backseat.

One of the features of the Trump Marina Hotel Casino in Atlantic City, besides numerous slot machines stamped with Donald Trump's face on the side, is an outdoor bar called the Deck that overlooks the bay and would soon be playing host to the Brides.

The musicians unloaded the van and carried their bags into the casino. Kerry Muldoon was already inside. Kerry has a button nose, thick brown hair cut in a shag, and a spunky, detail-oriented personality. She was listening intently as the event promoter, a guy named Al Faucera, ran down the itinerary. The band was to play two sets: at 4:30 P.M. and again at 9:30 P.M. A local classic rock station, WMGM 103.7 "the Shark," was sponsoring the concert, which also featured a Led Zeppelin tribute (Get the Led Out) and a Foreigner band (Head Games). Al explained that it was a yearly event called Fake Fest. This year happened to be Fake Fest III.

Maurice seemed to find the name objectionable. *"Fake Fest?"* he said to Al, sounding offended.

"Let me show you guys your dressing room," Al said cheerily, leading everyone across the noisy casino floor, up an escalator, and to a dingy room the size of a walk-in closet that the Brides were sharing with the other tribute bands. Some of the guys from the Zeppelin tribute were already inside; the Robert Plant was standing in front of the mirror, putting on a frilly purple blouse.

Outside, a crowd of middle-aged guys wearing khaki shorts, sunglasses, and sandals stood at the bar drinking beer out of plastic cups as the DJ from 103.7 the Shark played classic rock hits like

"Baba O'Riley" by The Who and Grand Funk Railroad's "We're an American Band." On a boardwalk overlooking the marina, a stage had been assembled with a thatch roof of the sort you might see on a Hawaiian beach. The Brides were headlining the evening show and going on second in the afternoon, following the Foreigner tribute band. Just after 4:30 P.M., they took the stage. Right off, without any introduction, the band launched into "Brown Sugar." Everyone stood, flat-footed, as Maurice, dressed in a lime-colored polka-dot shirt, white sneakers, and black leather pants a size too tight, danced and belted the melody. When the song ended, he spoke to the crowd for the first time. "Here we are again in Atlantic City," he said, leaning on the microphone stand and taking a familiar tone, as if he were a local celebrity making his big return. "Land of boxing, gambling, bikini tops, and big old giant-ass boats right over there." He motioned to the yachts dotting the marina and, in a sassy voice, said, "Who can afford those things? They're so *massive.*" Pause. "This one's called 'Honky Tonk Women.' Play it, Daniel."

Daniel played the song's famous two-chord opening and the crowd cheered in recognition. Then the band members all fell in. They were seasoned musicians and looked totally in control, like someone who had been on a stretch of road a thousand times before and knew every turn. The lead guitarist, Lee Boice, was an especially good player; his fingers moved across the fretboard with an effortless precision while he chewed gum and looked at the crowd and struck his best nonchalant pose. But the musicians were supporting players. It was Maurice's show: he commanded the stage with the haughty swagger of an old-school R&B showman, dictating the songs, the mood, the tempo, yelling when he wanted the band to play louder or faster, singing in a big full-throated voice. Between songs he kept up a steady banter with the audience: "We've never rehearsed this one. This is what we like to do, get dangerous. . . . 'Stray Cat Blues' for the brother who shouted that out. . . . You young guys digging this? Yeeeaaah, this is what your parents went to see when they were young. Messed-up, ain't it? They was all jacked up on some things we don't want to get into right now. . . . Hold on. Let me see that. Now *that's* a hickey. . . . Ooooh, look at this girl here. She got those fine-ass little titties. She turnin' red. Don't be embarrassed. I like little titties. . . . This one's called 'Can't Always Get What You Want'. . . . So y'all going to see the Stones? For the eight hundred and twelfth time? *Goddamn.* Them mothers just won't die, will they? First time I seen people already embalmed and still walkin' round."

At first, the crowd was stiff and self-conscious, but with each song, Maurice lured more people onto the boardwalk, until, midway through the first set, the dance area was filled with people clapping and singing. Even a shy, overweight Goth girl began to dance after Maurice jumped off the stage, pulled her onto the boardwalk, kissed her on the cheek, then jumped onstage again. *"Got-to-get-it, got-to-get-it, got-to-get-it, got-to-get-it, got-to-get-it, got-to-get-it, yeah,"* he sang as the band stretched out the refrain. "Satisfaction. *Come on!* I need some satisfaction." By the force of his will, he had created a lively party from nothing. Later that night, he did it again, as he'd been doing for the last twenty-five years.

5

Sticky Fingers plays about fifty concerts a year, and the majority
of them, in dingy fraternity house basements or half-empty rock
clubs, tend to reinforce the fact that the band members are pretend rock stars rather than actual ones. Occasionally, however,
they land a gig that delivers the very rock star glamour they are
simulating. In 2001, Sticky Fingers flew to Moscow to perform at
the opening of a club there called Voodoo Lounge. Glen brought
Julia along, and they stayed in a hotel near the Kremlin, toured
the city, and drank champagne with the Russian club owner. A
year later, the band scored a weeklong residency at the Hard
Rock Hotel in Bali, Indonesia, and spent the week playing music
and partying on the beach. Some foreign engagements haven't
gone as smoothly. Once, Glen brought a Keith who looked nothing like Keith Richards to a gig in Central America, and the club

owners became angry and said they had been cheated. On another occasion, the band performed at a classic rock festival in Canada on the same bill with Foreigner, April Wine, and Alice Cooper, but after Canadian taxes Glen returned home owing money. Still, you couldn't say it had been a bust; Sticky Fingers had played for a crowd of thousands on the same stage as Alice Cooper!

During the year I followed the band, Glen was contacted by the promoter of an event called Tribute Band Night—a spectacular concert that takes place each year in the Netherlands, featuring tribute bands from around the world. That year's concert was being held on June 18 at the Ahoy arena in Rotterdam, and would include tributes to Blondie; U2; Earth, Wind & Fire; Pink Floyd; and ABBA. The promoter said he wanted a Rolling Stones band, too. Sticky Fingers was going to Europe.

One sunny Friday a few weeks before the Rotterdam concert, I traveled with the band to a more routine engagement—a party at the Sigma Alpha Epsilon fraternity house at Washington and Lee University in Lexington, Virginia. Transportation matters for Sticky Fingers tended to be convoluted, especially since Glen had moved to Florida and no longer drove the band to shows in his Dodge van, as he had in years past. On this trip, Dan and the fill-in bassist, Alex, were driving in Dan's car, while Glen was driving up from Florida and I was taking Kevin Gleeson and George Steckert in my car. When I picked Kevin up that morning, he was standing on lower Broadway in Manhattan, already Keithed up in a pair of tight jeans, a blue snap-button shirt, a black vest, and sunglasses. Driving on I-78 through Pennsylvania two hours later, with George riding shotgun and Kevin sprawled across the backseat, smoking a cigarette, his shirt unbuttoned to expose his skinny chest, I had the odd feeling I was chauffeuring Keith Richards around the eastern seaboard.

I was always amazed at how completely Kevin inhabited the role of Keith. On road trips, he would arrive dressed as Richards and remain in costume until he returned home. The few times I saw him dressed normally he appeared profoundly uncomfortable, as if he weren't himself unless he was wearing a pair of leather pants and a shark-tooth necklace. One day, I had the chance to watch Kevin change before a show. He seemed to approach the task not as a way to become someone else, but as a means to become his true self. We were in a Days Inn in Alabama, and Kevin sat shirtless in front of the mirror, his costume spread out on the counter before him. There was a clear process at work, and he narrated as he went. The first step was to put on a black leather headband—the one adorned with African beads, a silver ring, a cross, a subway token, a clump of his own hair. "I pull it all the way down and then with a comb I bring my hair out over it," he said, fitting the headpiece snug, like a wig. "It's all my own hair. That way, there's no donor rejection." He let out a bronchial, wheezy laugh. After he ran a pick through his hair so that it frizzed out over the headband in all directions like a fright wig, he took a small plastic bottle, poured blue liquid onto a cloth, and began scrubbing his face. "I have a special alcohol scrub I put on," he said. "It's got salicylic acid. It comes from Avon. I buy more Avon than my wife." He scrubbed vigorously along his jawline. "You got to clean your face real good so you get a good shine in the lights." He grabbed a makeup pencil and carefully worked around his eyes. "I got this special mascara for men. I try not to use too much. Too much, you look like Ozzy." He worked the pencil. "The current Keith doesn't use much makeup, but Glen wants me to look like seventies Keith," he said. "The secret is smudging. Smudging is why we get the big bucks in Sticky Fingers." He laughed his wheezy laugh again. Then he stood up and put on a teal button-up blouse. When he turned around, he was *full-on Keef.*

On the drive to Washington and Lee, I asked Kevin how he was adjusting to being back in New York again.

He said he was staying at his mother's studio apartment in Queens and settling into his job with the police department. It turned out one of the desk sergeants was the John Lennon in the Beatles tribute band Strawberry Fields; he and Kevin took smoke breaks together. "There's a sense of humor involved in all of this," Kevin said, flicking his ash out the window. "All the years I was a junkie—today, I work for the cops." The only drawback of his new job, he said, besides missing his family back in Chicago, was that he wasn't able to go on the road during the week. "You can't tell the police, 'I'm going off to play Keith Richards. I'll be back on Monday,' " Kevin said.

At one point, Kevin and I switched places and he took the wheel. As he drove, he chain-smoked and regaled George and me with tales of his junkie days. The stories, each one more harrowing than the last, had a fantastical quality to them. He said he was a drug addict from 1977, when he was seventeen, to 1986, when he entered rehab. During those years, he said, he had a five-bag-a-day habit and was living with strippers who brought home Hefty bags full of Quaaludes. He said his veins were abscessed and he weighed 109 pounds. I once asked Kevin's younger sister, Colleen, about his drug use, and she said she couldn't remember it being that bad, but Kevin said that all he did in those years was shoot heroin and play Delta blues guitar. "I wanted to go back to the crossroads to find Satan and make my deal," he said. "I lived on potatoes and sugar water. And Jell-O and popcorn. And Listerine and Cracker Jacks."

"Potatoes and sugar water?" George said. "What's that about?"

Kevin paused, as if searching for the correct answer. "Easy to cook," he said finally. "You can't fuck up a potato. And water is free, comes from the tap. So between starch, potassium, and glucose, you stay alive." There was pride in his voice, as though he felt he had lived the rock and roll life and survived, like Keith Richards. "In the shooting galleries in Alphabet City," he went on incredibly, "the junkies stacked the bodies of people who overdosed near the door so the police would trip over them during raids. I've been stabbed. I've been locked in a supply closet and beaten to a pulp. I didn't start imitating Keith until 2000. With me, half of it ain't even imitating. I know it sounds like I'm braggin', man. The thing is, your life is a series of stories of what you can remember, and this is what I did."

George nodded noncommittally. When it came to talking about himself, George tended to be much less expansive. I knew from bits of conversation here and there that he'd grown up in Sayreville, New Jersey, the same town Jon Bon Jovi is from, and after high school attended Franklin Pierce University, which he chose mainly because it's in the same state—New Hampshire— where the members of Aerosmith, his favorite band, met. After college, George moved to Key West, which he calls "a sunny place for shady people." He spent a year there working as a barker at a go-go bar called Rum Runners; then he joined a high school buddy near Fort Lauderdale and they both got jobs delivering plants. I once asked him to tell me about his days in Florida, and he said, "That was a crazy time. My friend Steve Dimato and I drove around in a blue seventy-two Thunderbird with broken lights that would blink on and off. We used to go to clubs and pick up girls. We went to the Squeeze, the club where Marilyn Manson hung out." When George returned to New Jersey, in 1993, he worked briefly at the brokerage firm Cantor Fitzgerald, in the World Trade Center. But he hated office life and quit to do odd jobs and play music, sometimes in bands, sometimes as a solo lounge act in bars along the Jersey shore. A friend of his had been playing bass in Sticky Fingers; when he left, George took his place. With his long hair and lean build, George looked most naturally like a rock star, especially when he wore his leather jacket and aviator sunglasses. He was popular with women, and for many years had lived with a girlfriend, but they'd recently split and now he was sharing a little place near the shore with a roommate and trying to save for a new used car. He always seemed to be scraping by financially.

I asked George how things were going since I'd seen him last at the show in Queens.

"It's cool, man," he said, and explained that he'd taken a job painting houses near his home, which allowed him to surf in the mornings. Then he stared out the window dreamily, as though picturing himself gliding through the breakers. "I'm all about self-propelled motion," he said. The conversation turned to the show in Rotterdam. Both Kevin and George were excited to fly to Europe and perform in an arena in front of so many people. It put George in mind of a photograph he'd once seen of Led Zeppelin in concert. In the photo, the band is onstage in an open-air stadium, and for as far as the image extends is a sea of people. "I want a picture of me onstage like that in Rotterdam," George said.

It turned out to be alumni weekend at Washington and Lee, and when we pulled into the frat house driveway that evening, Sigma Alpha Epsilon alums were mingling on the colonnaded porch. Practically everyone was dressed in the same outfit—khaki pants, white oxford shirt, blue blazer—except the women, who wore print dresses. The frat house itself sat at the top of a wide, tree-dotted hill and had the air of an old plantation. Dan was already in the frat's basement party room when we got there, setting up his drums on a wooden stage. Kevin began the sacred task of unpacking his guitars: a blond maple-wood Fender Telecaster with a black pick guard; a black Tele with a humbucker in the bridge position. Both configured for five-string, open G tuning, and, according to Kevin, both outfitted with the same string gauges (.011, .015, .018, .030, and .042) and strings (Ernie Ball Nickel Wound) that Keith Richards uses. The blond Tele was for "Honky Tonk Women," "Brown Sugar," "Can't You Hear Me Knocking," "Start Me Up," and "Wild Horses"; the black one, capo'd at the fourth fret, for "Tumbling Dice," "Jumpin' Jack Flash," "Happy," and "Street Fighting Man." And for songs in standard tuning—a 1970s G&L Tele with a swamp ash body and blond maple neck, white pearl pick guard, and two P-90 "soapbar" pickups. (Kevin owns ten guitars and carried no less than four to gigs, slung over his shoulder, Sherpa-like, in a homemade carrying contraption.)

Soon Glen arrived. He wore a white oxford shirt, jeans, and scuffed penny loafers. His mood was buoyant. "Wait until you hear about this hottie I met down in Florida," he said right off.

"She's the daughter of the former governor, Lawton Chiles. Looks just like Angelina Jolie."

I was accustomed to hearing Glen's enthusiasms. He was possessed of the strident cheer of an incorrigible dreamer. Each time I saw him, he was brimming with some piece of good news: a promoter had called and wanted to book Sticky Fingers for a series of big shows, or a famous record producer had heard his demo and been impressed. In many instances, the leads never panned out, but sometimes they did, like the Rotterdam concert. Presented with one stroke of good fortune, Glen's mind naturally turned several revolutions. In the case of the Rotterdam show, Glen said that if the event promoter was pleased he might invite the band back each year, or connect them with other booking agents in Europe. "We could bring the boys over every summer and do the music festivals," Glen said. "Next thing you know, we're touring Europe."

Just then, a clean-cut, sandy-haired frat brother approached the stage and introduced himself as the entertainment director.

Dan said to the frat brother, whose name was Mike, "I think we've played here before. I recall a group of sorority girls who were drunk and became very friendly with the band." He grinned.

"That was bid week, my freshman year," Mike said. He was a junior now, and it occurred to me that Sticky Fingers has been a fixture in the college life of four cycles of southern undergraduates.

Glen, always at home in a campus setting, initiated a discussion with Mike on the virtues of sorority girls. "Enjoy these times," I heard him saying in a tone of fatherly advisement. Then he disappeared into the frat house laundry room to change for the show.

A word here about Sticky Fingers concerts: the band's performances are sometimes tight and punchy, or loose and boister-
ous, or dissonant, or tuneful, or filled with all the exultant joy of
rock and roll, or a complete drunken mess, but rarely are they
boring. Mostly, this is because of Glen, who in his performing
style is like a punk rocker—raw and erratic and inviting of chaos.
George once called Glen "the Ayatollah of rock 'n' rolla." Dan
once said to me, "I'll swear up and down that Glen is not a good
singer. He'll probably agree to that. But as an entertainer, he's
Tom Jones. He's Elvis. When he's onstage, the show is *happening.*"
At a Sticky Fingers show, the imaginary boundary that separates
the performer and the audience is gleefully destroyed. The result
is a thrilling sense that anything can happen. Once, at a wedding
reception the band played, I turned briefly away from the stage,
and when I looked back, Glen had abandoned the microphone
and was on the floor, dirty-dancing with the bride. At another
show, a girl in the crowd walked onstage, grabbed Dan's drumsticks, and, without a word, began to drum on "Honky Tonk
Women."

Generally speaking, the band's shows do adhere to a *loose*
narrative arc. Often, they begin with an up-tempo tune, like
"Brown Sugar" or "Start Me Up," and follow with fifteen or so of
the Stones' biggest hits. (The only hit you will almost never hear
is "Beast of Burden," which for mysterious reasons Glen dislikes
and has forbidden the band to play.) At some point, Glen will exit
the stage and Kevin will sing a few Keith numbers, like "Happy"
or "Little T&A." He introduced the mini-set as a treat for fans,
but he approaches the selection of material with the myopia of a
Stones obsessive, and as a result, the songs are often so obscure—
unreleased demos, rare B sides, old R&B numbers that Keith

once covered live—that most people don't know them, including the other band members.

The second set can take any number of directions, depending on how much Glen has had to drink during the break. If, say, he has finished off a bottle of Southern Comfort, he will most likely decide he wants to play drums. This used to infuriate Dan, but he's inured to it and uses the time to towel off and drink a beer while Glen bashes away joyfully. Following this, there will often be a sloppy version of the slow blues "Little Red Rooster" and a rendition of "Midnight Rambler" that captures remarkably the song's dark and violent energy, with Glen wailing feverishly on the harmonica and screaming about sticking his knife right down your throat. If the band is playing at a fraternity, by now a group of frat brothers will have ambled onstage. Hoisting their beers in the air, they will sing off-key and look out at their friends with an amazed expression that, roughly translated, says, *Dude, I'm onstage with the band!*

That night at Washington and Lee, all of these things happened, more or less in that order. The band kicked off the concert with a crisp version of "Start Me Up," Dan's drumming working in lockstep with Kevin's and George's chunky guitar rhythms. Soon the fraternity brothers and sorority girls began to dance in the style peculiar to southern undergraduates—a sort of fox-trot that is surprisingly chaste and old-fashioned, as though tight jeans and the bump 'n' grind were never invented. After Sticky Fingers had played a number of songs, George stepped to the microphone and said, "All right, Washington and Lee, consider yourself fingered!" For the Keith fans, Kevin dusted off a long-forgotten/never-remembered song called "We Had It All." The college kids stopped dancing and stared blankly at the band. After a short break and a fair amount of whiskey, Glen emerged from the dressing room wearing a tipsy grin and a mesh football jersey imprinted with the letters SAE. Then he told the college kids, "If you drink and drive, drive home fast." A group of drunken frat brothers at the foot of the stage roared. Sticky Fingers played a loose and sweaty second set and ended with a rousing version of "Midnight Rambler." Just after 1:00 A.M., the college kids filed out of the frat house basement, leaving its floor sticky with spilled beer.

A scene from the Continental Airlines international departures counter in Newark Liberty International Airport at around 6:45 on the evening of Friday, June 17, 2005: a skinny, very sweaty man lugging two guitar cases and a backpack rushes up to a ticket attendant and pleads to be let onto the 7:00 P.M. flight to Amsterdam. The attendant explains that it's too late to catch that flight. The man begs, then asks to see a supervisor and begs some more. The supervisor relents and provides the man with a golf cart and a driver to whisk him to the gate. Speeding through the airport, the man hastily changes into snakeskin boots, a bandanna, scarves, a hairpiece, and makeup, turning himself into Keith Richards as airline passengers look on in bewilderment.

When Kevin finally arrived at the airport gate (he'd raced from his job with the police department), he was joined by an alternate version of Sticky Fingers. Weeks earlier, Glen had decided to take to Rotterdam what he described to me as his "A team"— the musicians he felt would make the best impression on the promoter. The A team consisted of Kevin as Keith, George on bass instead of guitar, a guy from New Jersey named Steve on rhythm guitar, and a drummer who'd apparently done studio session work in Nashville. Dan was noticeably absent from the A team. For two years, he had been the band's drummer and de facto tour manager, putting thousands of miles on his car and often fronting travel expenses out of his own pocket. But he would not be going to Rotterdam. In fact, he didn't know Sticky Fingers was playing the concert (Glen had sworn Kevin and George to secrecy) and wasn't told about it until later, after it had already taken place.

I didn't go to Rotterdam, either, because my work schedule did not permit it. I wished I could have gone, though, because a tribute band festival is a surreal and mind-altering experience. All the musicians hang out backstage and trade stories, and after a while you start to feel as if you have entered a parallel rock and roll universe, peopled not by Mick Jagger or Bono or Axl Rose but by their tribute doppelgängers. I did hear about the trip from everyone who went, though, and Kevin later wrote me a letter about the experience, which said, in part:

> Glen was in a severely good mood on the flight. The stewardesses were fascinated with us and flirted all the way across the ocean trying to find out where we were staying, playing and when we were returning home. Glen was at the top of his game, spinning yarns and tales of adventures in rock and roll and showmanship. After 6 hours the plane swung low over fields and farms and windmills and touched down at Amsterdam's main airport. The guitars appeared, as did our driver, the limo van, and customs officials, and we were flying down a Netherlands superhighway looking at windmills, tulips, small cars, trucks. It was a sunny morning. The van filled with all sorts of smoke and laughter, everyone, including the promoters, happy that the ragtag American band

made it. The driver, in perfect English, gave us details—i.e. itinerary, food, sleep, free time, sound
check times, concert hall info. We drove to Rotterdam to the Hilton 5 star. Our luggage was taken and
delivered, we were fed, given rooms and let loose on
the city. After freshening up, Glen, George and I
headed for the city Market for shopping and brows-
ing. They were looking for the smoke shops. Glen
and I were looking for Moroccan prayer shawls and
belts and boots. We ate and found the smoke shops.
We went upstairs. Glen and George saddled up to
the bar and proceeded to get tongue-hanging-out
stoned. I took up position along a far wall to assist
with getting them back downstairs. Outside, we met
guys and girls who came with other bands from Ger-
many (ABBA) and the U.K. (U2 and Queen). We had 5
hours till sound check. We had arrived the day of the
show and were adjusting to the time difference. We
ate at a McDonald's which served Big Macs on pita
bread and fries with a green sauce.

Later that day, the band was driven to the Ahoy arena, where
they were led onstage to do a sound check and the staging cues
were explained, like the pyrotechnic display of shooting flames
that would accompany their performance. Kevin wrote:

Then instructions about dress, look, motivation, effect and flashlights, leading us back thru the tunnels,
and labyrinths of wires and boards and down the
gangplanks and back up into the backstage safety of
the dressing rooms, and dress, and makeup, and
hair, and going over guitar parts while the four other
acts did their sound checks. And then we hear it, the
noise 11,000 people make when they want to hear
music, and suddenly there's no time to be nervous
anymore because the lady with the headset and clipboard is leading us and pointing and saying "go, go,
go." I step up and strike *da-dah dah* and close my

eyes as a wall of flame envelops me, as 40 concussion bombs go off. I open my eyes and the drums slap in and the lights come up and the crowd surges forward to the barricades and barriers and everyone knows we are here to party and then Glen is singing "Start Me Up" and 11,000 people are going ape shit. Behind us the two girls from the ABBA tribute are singing "You make a grown man cry," and deafening applause. I'm aware of George behind me on bass and we smile at the intensity of it all. Glen saunters over to me, looks me right in the eye, and we share a smile knowing that this is the shit, and he rests his head on my shoulder and gives the cameras a glimpse of Mick and Keith at home working. He smiles and gallivants off across the stage while I turn and head back to the drums to line up for the end of the song, which we nail as all the lights go out.

A month after the Rotterdam concert, I saw Sticky Fingers perform on a balmy Friday night at a bar on the north shore of Long Island. Kevin and George were still marveling at the experience of performing in a crowded arena in Europe. "The comedown was *intense*," George said.

We were all leaning against a wooden rail on the bar's second-story back porch. It was a balmy night and George was dressed in a loose beach-style print shirt. "Now I understand why rock stars do drugs—to keep that feeling going," he said. "All week after I came back, I was daydreaming about playing in front of thousands of people."

I ended up seeing some of the Rotterdam concert after all, by way of a promotional DVD that Glen put together from edited footage shot by a film crew. I could understand why the experience had remained with them. Sticky Fingers had been the first band to play, and when Kevin hit the opening riff to "Start

Me Up," flames shot thirty feet into the air, illuminating the arena. Eleven thousand screaming fans cheered. Flanking either side of the stage were the very same gigantic inflatable dolls that the Stones had used on the *Steel Wheels* tour. By the end of the band's short set, Glen was bare-chested and wearing his white football pants and a cape fashioned from American and British flags tied together; he blew a kiss to the crowd and bowed exultantly.

Kevin and George didn't say much more about the Rotterdam concert that night. I gathered it was because Dan was standing nearby, and perhaps they felt guilty about his not going along. I brought this point up with George once, and he shrugged and said, "I feel shitty about it, but what can I do? It's Glen's band." Months later, after Dan and Glen had another falling-out over a separate matter, I asked Dan if he was hurt that he had not been invited to Rotterdam, and he said, "I was upset about that, I admit I would have liked to go to Europe," then dropped the subject.

The week following the Rotterdam show—and with Dan back on drums—Sticky Fingers played in Atlanta and returned to perform there the next week. And they had been flown to Southern California to perform in front of six thousand people at a town fair. After years of instability, Sticky Fingers had a steady lineup again, and the members were beginning to gel musically. There was, that night on Long Island, a renewed sense of purpose among the band. Dan had begun using silver-colored Streaks 'N Tips spray to look more Charlie Watts–like. And instead of his usual Southern Comfort, Glen sipped from a Dasani water bottle. His sleeveless black muscle shirt revealed newly toned biceps. "I've been working out ever since I met this chick a few weeks ago in Miami," he said.

I asked if this was the Angelina Jolie look-alike, the one whose father was the former governor of Florida.

"No, no," Glen said. "This chick is British. Lisa. You've got to see this woman," he said, and he winced, as if Lisa's physical gifts could cause a man pain. Then he lowered his voice to a near whisper and said, "I think I may be in love."

The band members stood around on the porch, talking idly and waiting for the opening act, a Frank Sinatra impersonator, to finish his set. Soon, the club manager appeared and said the Sinatra guy was almost done and that Sticky Fingers would go on shortly. It was a warm-up date for the band: in a month the Stones tour would kick off in Boston, and Sticky Fingers' schedule would go into high gear, as the band followed the Stones across the country, playing tie-in shows. On the eve of the tour there was a palpable excitement in the air, as though a thrilling adventure was about to begin.

"Okay," Glen said, suddenly serious. "No noodling on your instruments between songs. No fooling around onstage. We're gonna go out there and bang, bang through the set tonight. Like professionals."

6

The Rolling Stones first toured America in 1964, with mixed re-
sults: they stayed for two and a half weeks and performed along
with rodeo riders at the Texas Teen Fair in San Antonio; saw
B. B. King live at a blues club on the South Side of Chicago;
recorded at the legendary Chess Studios; were ridiculed by Dean
Martin during an appearance on the TV show *The Hollywood
Palace;* and spent the rest of the tour playing to half-empty auditoriums. At the time, the Stones had released just one album and
were popular on both coasts but unknown in the rest of the
country. Nor did the Stones know much about America; according to Stanley Booth's book about the band, *Dance with the Devil,*
when the Stones played Hershey, Pennsylvania, they were puz-
zled as to why the buildings were painted brown and there was
chocolate everywhere.

The Stones returned to America again that year, then toured twice in 1965, but it wasn't until 1969 that Stones tours grew into the ballyhooed events they are now. On the '69 tour, the Stones were in what many consider their golden period—a four-year burst of creativity from 1968 to 1972, when the band recorded and released *Beggars Banquet, Let It Bleed, Sticky Fingers,* and the double album *Exile on Main Street.* It was on the '69 tour, during a concert at Madison Square Garden, that the Stones recorded *Get Yer Ya-Ya's Out,* one of the great live albums in rock. It was also on that tour that the Stones held a free concert at the Altamont Speedway, not far from San Francisco. The Stones envisioned the event as a West Coast Woodstock, but they hired the Hells Angels motorcycle gang as security, which in retrospect wasn't a very sound idea and resulted in a young black man in the audience being fatally stabbed by one of the Angels. The concert and the brutal killing were captured in the documentary film *Gimme Shelter,* and the band received a lot of negative media attention, but the publicity only seemed to add to the Stones' allure as rock outlaws.

In the following decade, the Stones toured America once every three years, usually in the summers. The tours became *the* music event of the season: radio stations held ticket giveaways and rock magazines like *Creem* and *Circus* ran articles ("Stones: Live at Last!") and interviews with the band ("Jagger Talks on Touring—First '75 Concert Photos & a Decade of Rare Pix"). In a way, the tours served as mileposts in the band's career, which is so protracted it can be broken into distinct periods, like geological ages. The '69 tour was the first without founding guitarist Brian Jones, who drowned in his swimming pool that July under mysterious circumstances. By 1972, the Stones had become jet-set rock and roll aristocrats, and the band traveled from city to city in a private plane with the red tongue and lips logo on the fuselage; *Rolling Stone* dispatched Truman Capote to write about the tour. The '75 "tour of the Americas" was the first with Ronnie Wood, and also the first to feature elaborate production elements, like the lotus stage that unfolded to reveal a band member in each petal and the twenty-foot-tall inflatable phallus. The '78 tour almost didn't happen because a year earlier Keith Richards was found with heroin in Toronto and charged with drug trafficking; Richards faced a prison sentence of seven years to life, but at the eleventh hour, a blind girl came forward and told the presiding judge that Richards had arranged for her safe transport to and from Stones shows, and the judge agreed to release him on the condition that he play a benefit concert for the blind.

It's easy to see how the tribute band musicians could get seduced by the notion of wanting to be in the Rolling Stones. When I was in college, and at the height of a period in which I wanted to be a rock musician, I spent hours fantasizing about being in a band like the Stones. I would look at pictures of the musicians onstage or sweeping through an airport or on holiday in some glamorous locale like Morocco and imagine leading a life as grand and adventurous and uncompromising as the Stones had—and then have it all captured in beautifully composed photographs. If I found myself in a situation that caused anxiety—attending a party where I knew no one, say, or flying for the first time—as a coping mechanism I sometimes pretended I was Keith Richards: emotionally disengaged, steely, the image of cool. With the exception of the Beatles, no other rock band has a richer narrative than the Stones. Part of being a Stones fan is appreciating the band's music, but an equal part is being seduced by the mythology: jet-setting tours, scrapes with the law, drug use, glamorous girlfriends, backstage parties, an ever-present gang of friends and celebrity hangers-on. Like many fans, Stones fans have their own language—a shared lexicon of images, sounds, and stories. Like Mick Jagger's famous quip to a female reporter who asked if he was satisfied: "Do you mean *sexually* or philosophically?" Or the creation tale of how Keith Richards came up with the riff to "Satisfaction": one night, half-asleep in a Florida hotel room, he played his guitar into a recorder and rewound the tape the next day to hear twenty minutes of snoring and then *dunt, dunt, da-da-da*. Or the dramatic image of the band piling into a dangerously overweighted helicopter and flying away from the bloody ground at Altamont. The band's story has the epic sweep of a great novel and the salacious detail of a trashy paperback. My favorite period in the band's history surrounds their decision to become tax exiles from England and move in the summer of 1971 to the French Riviera. Keith Richards rented a sprawling old house there called Villa Nellcote, where he threw lavish parties and entertained houseguests like Terry Southern and the singer-songwriter Gram Parsons, and trolled the Riviera in a yacht he named the *Mandrax,* after a type of downer. The Stones recorded one of rock's greatest albums, *Exile on Main Street,* in the villa's sweltering basement. Richards was twenty-seven years old; Mick Jagger turned twenty-eight that summer. Speaking of the period that led up to Nellcote, Richards's longtime paramour, the German model Anita Pallenberg, once said, "For a few years then we were just flying. We had everything—money, power, looks, protection. We had the lot."

One Friday in mid-August, nine days before the opening night of the Stones tour, I drove to Cape Cod to see the Blushing Brides perform at a club there. I was curious to see the Brides in Massachusetts, where the band had always been popular and where they still had many fans from the old days. Also, I wanted to see the Brides before they disappeared for a few months. Apparently, New England was not big enough for both "the World's Most Dangerous Tribute to the Music of the Rolling Stones" and the actual Stones, because Maurice was going on hiatus until the tour passed through. When I arrived at the club, a long and low-slung building on Route 28, the main road along the southern Cape, the air was balmy and a thick fog had rolled in. In the parking lot a bright neon sign read:

THE SPEAKEASY
Restaurant–Show Club–Flair Bar

Tonite
BLUSHING BRIDES
STONES TRIBUTE
KIDS EAT FREE!

When I walked in, a few guys were seated at a square-shaped bar, watching a Red Sox game on TV, and two dozen more were in the back room, sitting at tables along the edge of a scuffed wooden dance floor, but overall the place had a big, empty, lonely feeling, like a summer resort in the off-season. The Brides were already into their set, playing a swinging version of "Little Queenie," the Chuck Berry song that the Stones sometimes covered in concert. At one point, Maurice leapt off the stage and stood in the center of the room, showily listening to the sound mix. By request, the band played "Shattered." Two little boys chased each other around the empty dance floor. A grandfatherly man softly tapped his foot. Then a woman and her young son got up and walked out to dance. "That's it, girl. Get on the dance floor," Maurice said as the band held down the rhythm. "Anyone else?" No one moved. The band finished "Shattered" and Maurice addressed the audience, focusing on a group he seemed to know sitting near the stage.

"Are y'all having fun?" he asked a little sarcastically. There were soft hand claps. "Not a very powerful round of applause, but I'll take it, 'cause it's scary up here tonight." He exhaled loudly and leaned against the microphone stand. "Seeing as how we're such a quaint little group, let's introduce ourselves," he said, seemingly more interested in talking than singing. Then he went around the room, calling people out and making little jokes based on what they said, like a stand-up comic. "What's your name? . . . Jo Ann? Lovely. Jo Ann, are you the woman who wants to get greased up with me? I brought the K-Y. You bring the body." As the routine wore on, the other band members began to fidget. They stood awkwardly onstage or pretended to tune their instruments, waiting for their singer to get back to singing. Finally, Maurice turned and gave the band the cue and they started playing "Beast of Burden." He sang in a fiery voice, as if he were entertaining two thousand people, not two dozen, and during the guitar solo, he rooster-walked along the lip of the stage, his lips puckered like Jagger's, his coltish mouth turned down in an exaggerated scowl.

After the first set, the band members walked out to the loading dock behind the club and hung around and discussed the low turnout at that night's show. It was the middle engagement of a three-day trip around the state. The night before, the band had played in Faneuil Hall Marketplace, a shopping area in downtown Boston; the following night they were booked into a club near the Rhode Island border.

"It's brutal in there," Lee Boice, the lead guitarist, said. "It's like we're playing to cardboard cutouts."

"I knew we were in trouble when we pulled in and the parking lot was half-empty," Maurice said. He was sweaty from performing and, as if by throwing a switch, had dropped his cheeky stage persona. He said to me, "This place used to be a club called Christine's. It was a real happening joint. On a Friday night, the parking lot was so packed, you couldn't even get a spot." He toweled his head. "Christine's was always a big show for the Brides," he said ruefully. "I don't know what happened tonight."

Just then, a stocky guy wearing a Rolling Stones T-shirt came out of the club's back door and exchanged a friendly hello with Maurice and Shane McConnell, who was again sitting in with the band. His name was Joe Scammon, and he had been following the Brides since 1981, back when he was in high school. "I used to wait in line for hours to see the Brides play the Channel in Boston," Joe later told me. "At that point, I hadn't seen the Stones, so I didn't have anything to compare it to, but I was blown away by how much energy the Brides had. The first time I saw them, in this old supper club in Framingham, Maurice was swinging from a chandelier." The Brides had a lot of fans from the old days like Joe, especially in Massachusetts, and many of them still showed up whenever the band played nearby. During the passing years, they had grown up with the band, gotten married, had kids. Sometimes female fans would come to concerts— women who had been wild young rock chicks when Maurice first met them and were now middle-aged moms. Joe had continued to follow the band, and he was friendly with some of the new guys like Daniel Hoffenberg, but he seemed to miss the old Brides. "Daniel is a good guitar player—he's raw, like how the Stones sound live. But Paul Martin *was* Keith Richards," he told me. "Paul and Moe had this chemistry together that's probably never going to be duplicated."

That night, there was a different version of the band from the one that had played even a month earlier: after the show in Atlantic City, Larry Love, the bassist, quit. According to Larry, Maurice had sent the band members an E-mail message criticizing their musicianship and comparing them unfavorably with the old Brides. "I don't need this shit, bro," Larry told me. Larry said that in twenty years in bands, he'd never met a musician as egotistical as Maurice. (The fill-in bassist was a guy with slouchy posture named Kurt. Later that night at the Speakeasy, he met a couple of rock chicks and wanted to hang around the club after the gig and party. Maurice had spent a lifetime hanging around clubs and now preferred a good night's sleep, and I sensed Kurt was not long for the band. I never saw him again after that weekend.)

The second set was much livelier than the first. From years of fronting a band, Maurice knew how to work an audience, how to get people over their inhibitions and get them on the dance floor, having a good time despite themselves. When Daniel Hoffenberg started the slinky guitar intro to "Monkey Man," Maurice said, "We gonna play it sexy," and everyone danced with an extra spring in their step. At one point between songs, he said, "We used to have a saying in the old Brides, back when we traveled with our own sound equipment, and it went: 'If it's too loud, you're *too fucking old.*' I know y'all are from good rock and roll stock, so it's never too loud." The crowd cheered.

Maurice was playful and flattering to the audience, but all night he appeared visibly agitated with the band. Often, he would stand with his back to the room, facing the other musicians, and yell at Daniel Hoffenberg to play louder, or wave his arms wildly like a petulant orchestra conductor when he wanted Rodney Ledbetter to hit the cymbals. To my ears, the band sounded tight. During "Tumbling Dice," Maurice invited a woman onstage to sing, and while they repeated the lines "Got to roll me" and "Keep on rolling" in a call and response, the band played an instrumental line that rolled in on itself, beautifully echoing the lyrics. It was as moving a version as I'd ever heard. But Maurice still seemed annoyed. And when the set was finished and the band returned for an encore, his ire shifted focus. Leaning against the microphone stand, he said, "So who's going to see the Stones?"

Scattered cheers.

Maurice shook his head in disapproval. "They just keep taking you motherfuckers for all your money. How much are you paying for a ticket?"

Somebody shouted out, "Three hundred dollars."

"*Three hundred dollars!*" Maurice said, sounding insulted. "How much did you pay to get in here tonight? Ten dollars?" Very slowly, he said, "We kick the motherfucking Rolling Stones' asses live. We've been kicking their ass for twenty-seven years and not once did Jagger go, 'Thank you very much.' *Not once.*" At first, his tone had been playful, but he soon became more serious, and the other band members began to fidget again. "We play the music the way it's supposed to be played," Maurice went on. "We sweat. We kick some ass. We have some fun. We talk about sex. 'Cause that's what this music is about—sex and fun. And that's *it*! It's not about ripping you off for money." Somebody in the crowd whoo-hooed, but Maurice didn't notice. He was on a roll: "Shit, to go see that rich fuck Jagger dance around? I'll body-slam that puny motherfucker. Keep your money and come see the Blushing Brides." There was a lone hand clap. Maurice's body seemed to slacken and his tone grew confessional. "Whew. I feel better now that I got that out," he said. "I've been holding that in for years. That feels good. I feel reborn." He laughed sharply. Then he gave the cue to the band and sang another song written by Mick Jagger.

The next morning, after rousing themselves from bed, the band drove to a breakfast spot a few miles from the Speakeasy. As is the case with most night owl rock musicians, the guys in the Brides had over the years been in a lot of twenty-four-hour diners, eating eggs and toast at 3 A.M., and a sit-down breakfast had become a ritual, although the band's loyalty to the first meal of the day was generally not reciprocated by the establishments in which they chose to eat it. Usually, the hostess took one look at the band and stuck them in a far back corner. That morning, the band was seated in the table closest to the front door, the better to hurry them out once they were finished.

When the waitress came to take everyone's order, Maurice asked for plain hot water to soothe his throat. After the waitress left, Maurice brought up the low turnout at the Speakeasy. He said the owner of the club had told him at the end of the night that the club was closing down after that weekend. The owner had gone into debt to buy the place, and lost his shirt, but said he wanted the Brides to play there one last time. "I'm waiting there to get the band's money, and he's telling me this awful fucking depressing story about how he lost everything," Maurice said. "I'm thinking, Shit, man, you should probably pay your bills before you pay us. But I can't do a charity gig, either."

The conversation turned to a former band member—a guy named Shaky, whom everyone knew from having played the Greenwich Village bar circuit. From what I gathered, Shaky was a brilliant but notoriously undependable bassist who lived a semi-feral existence and was forever showing up late to gigs, or wandering off, or passing out onstage from lack of sleep.

"Is he still alive?" Shane said.

"Supposedly someone just saw him on Bleecker Street," Maurice said.

Shane shook his head in amazement. "I used to see him on Bleecker Street," he said. "It'd be, like, February, and Shaky would be walking around in a T-shirt, talking to himself." Shane appeared amused. "The only thing you could count on Shaky for was to never stop talking," he said. "Every town you passed through, he would have some obviously fictitious story about it. Like in the middle of the night you're driving and you pass some sign and it says, like, 'Podunckle.' Shaky would go"—here Shane's voice became manic in imitation—" 'Oh, yeah, Podunckle. I lived here from seventy-three to seventy-four. I was sleepin' with the mayor's daughter, 'cause she loved me, but I was tellin' her, no, I'm nothing but trouble, but she wouldn't not have me. So we're in her house, and I've got five pounds of pot that my friends gave me, and the SWAT team shows up, and I dig a tunnel under the house.' " Everyone who knew Shaky laughed in recognition at the impression. When the laughter stopped, Shane said, "The next day you're in Gulfchester and Shaky's like, 'Did I tell you about the time I played here with Ann-Margret?' "

"Yeah, but he's a great player," Lee Boice said in defense. Lee was a ruggedly handsome guy in his fifties, with dirty-blond hair worn in a rooster cut, à la Rod Stewart. He grew up in Jersey City, New Jersey, and gave off a "have guitar will travel" air, but his true passion was the sitar; he'd studied with Indian masters and recorded two world music albums that had found release in India. Lee said in his low, slow Jersey City baritone, "I used to jam with Shaky and this other cat, and together they knew about six thousand songs, man. One night, me, Shaky, and this guy are playing and they say, 'Let's do side B of the first Bee Gees record.' I'm like, *'Side B of the first Bee Gees record?* I don't know that.'"

Without looking up from his tea, Maurice said disdainfully, "The Bee Gees are so *white.*"

Shane looked to Maurice. "You're one of these guys who wished you were black, aren't you?" Shane was the only guy in the band who could challenge Maurice without reproach. Shane said, "You know, a lot of times I find I like the white versions of songs better than the black version."

Lee looked at Shane skeptically. "You mean like Pat Boone over Little Richard?"

"What about Johnny Winter?" Shane countered. "You can't get more white than an albino blues guitarist."

At the mention of Johnny Winter, all heads at the table bowed deferentially. "Johnny is some serious shit," Maurice said.

The waitress brought the food and set out the plates and silverware. When she left, Lee recounted the time he happened to be in the same Manhattan rehearsal studio as Winter, a legendary drinker. Lee said he'd watched, awestruck, as Johnny took an orange juice container, dumped out most of the juice, filled the container with vodka, then chugged. "I remember looking at him, going, *Wow,* this guy's going to be blasted in five seconds, man," Lee said. "Then he played another song and sounded great. I'm thinking, How the fuck is this guy even standing?"

"Talk about drunk," Shane said. "One time I saw Eddie Money at this club in Toronto. He was totally bombed, and he had this big snot booger on his face. Everybody in the club knew it but him. He's singing, and all I can see is this giant booger. It's just, like, *hanging there.* Finally, a roadie ran out with a rag and wiped it off his face."

One of the things I looked forward to most whenever I went on the road with the tribute bands was hearing the musicians tell stories. Being in a working band, you're constantly traveling, meeting new people, performing in different places, and you're doing it as a group, which tends to foster the telling and sharing of stories. The musicians have to tolerate countless hassles—fly-by-night promoters, flaky bandmates, a scrambling lifestyle of near poverty—but it seems to me that what they don't earn in money, or fame, or family comforts, they are rewarded in stories. Shane, especially, was a natural storyteller with a lifetime of kicking around in bands to draw on. In 1979, he moved from Sault Ste. Marie to Toronto with his first real band, Fahrenheit. Over the years, he had been in lots of bands, came close to signing a record deal a few times, watched some of his friends sign deals, moved to New York City, married and had a son, got divorced, played in more bands. For money, he had worked in restaurants, installed artwork in office buildings, cleaned apartments, been part of a demolition crew, delivered *Learning Annex* circulars, and scored sound tracks for pharmaceutical promotional videos. He had a million anecdotes filed away, and on long road trips he would re-count them, in his long-voweled Canadian accent, and entertain everyone as the miles passed.

Here are a few Shane stories:

"I Got Aerosmith Back Together"

"When I was playing with this band the Rockers, we once did a festival gig in Hamilton, outside of Toronto. Mountain was on the bill and a bunch of big Toronto bands, and also the Joe Perry Project. I was an Aerosmith freak, so after the show I went over to the band's trailer. Their road manager was there, so I go, 'Can I talk to Joe?' The manager goes, 'Sure, he's in there,' so I go in this trailer and it's just me and Joe. I was gonna leave after five min-utes, but I thought, You know what, he's not doing anything. I bet I could just sit here. So I sat there for, like, three hours while Joe smoked cigarettes and I asked him about cars and guitars. Cars and guitars—that's what he's into. For some reason, I asked him where he was staying, and he said, 'Oh, this Holiday Inn in Burlington.' So the next time I heard they were playing the area, I called that hotel. I said to the desk clerk, 'Can I have one of the rooms for the Joe Perry Project?' She said, 'Do you know which room? 'Cause I have four different rooms.' So I get connected to a room and I'm like, 'I'm looking for Greg, the road manager.' The guy goes, 'He's not here. Who's this?' I said, 'It's Shane.' He goes, 'Hey, Shane, it's Joe. I'll tell Greg to leave a couple of tickets at the door.' So I show up at the club and I go to the dressing room before the show and a guy at the door goes, 'You got any-thing?' I go, 'Yeah, I've got some pot.' He goes, 'That's for later. You can't come in unless you've got something that will get him up.' So I said, 'I'll come back.' Joe finished his show at, like, eleven P.M. That night, Aerosmith was playing with the two new guitar players down the road, in Toronto. After the show, I'm in the dressing room hanging out with Joe. I said, 'Your buddies are doing a show tonight right down the road. They might even still be playing.' He goes, 'What?' I said, 'Aerosmith. They're playing at the Garden tonight. Your hotel is in that direction. You should drop by and surprise them.' So that's the last I mention it. Twenty years later, I'm reading this book about Aerosmith and Steven Tyler is talking about how the band reunited. Tyler is saying, 'It all blew up, his wife hated mine, and I hadn't talked to Joe in two years. One day, out of nowhere, he just shows up at a gig in Toronto. I saw him and said, "It's so good to see you, man." ' At some point, there was a line in the book that said, 'Some guy told Joe that Aerosmith was playing in Toronto.' And I went, *I'm that guy! I'm that guy!* I got my favorite band in the universe back together."

"So I Went to a Loan Shark . . ."

"Some stories are just New York stories because you don't really go on the road here. You're in a band, but you're in New York the whole time. I was playing with this girl and she had a deal with a big record company and a woman manager. It turned out to be almost a development deal 'cause there was only some money and you weren't getting a release on your album. You had a deal, but you were still always fighting to get what you wanted. So this girl's manager starts to feel like she needs to make some kind of big move to make things happen. The manager calls the people who are promoting a Black Crowes tour on the East

Coast. She says, 'What do I need to do to get my opening band a slot on this Black Crowes tour?' On most tours, there's already an opening band, but if you want to work a deal, you can sometimes *open* for the opening band. I remember when Tina Turner was huge, this Canadian band, Glass Tiger, had to pay, like, half a million dollars to get on the European leg of the tour. That's great exposure. So anyway, it's gonna be a couple of nights at the Beacon, somewhere around Boston, and somewhere else. Three or four shows—and it's gonna cost, like, fifteen grand. I'm the guitar player. It's only the singer and me, and we hire other people to do stuff with us. But the singer hasn't told us about any of this yet. It seems like over this one week she's really edgy. Finally, we're at her place one day and she's distraught and she breaks down. She says, 'I'm doing these four gigs with the Black Crowes and it's gonna cost me fifteen thousand dollars to make it happen, seven or eight grand up front. So I went to a loan shark and borrowed fifteen thousand dollars.' She gets the money from the loan shark, gives the promoter half the money, puts the other half in a drawer in her room. Now the only people who even go into her apartment are me, the singer, her best friend—this girl she's known for fifteen years—and her vocal coach, who works at the most renowned voice doctor place in the world. This guy was President Clinton's voice doctor on the road when he was campaigning. He's the only guy who's in her apartment besides her best friend and us two. And the money goes missing. She's like, 'Would my best friend take the money? Would Dr. Bill take the money?' I didn't even know anything about the money. At the time, the singer set me up living in an apartment with her best friend. The singer is telling me, 'I can't do these shows because I can't pay the rest of the money to the promoter, and he's not giving me back my deposit, and now I have a loan shark calling me. I think I'm going to have to leave the continent.' So the next day, she calls me and says, 'When my friend goes to work, trash her room and look for the money.' I'm going, 'What are you talking about? *I'm living in the other room.* What if she comes home?' So next thing I know, I'm on the phone, rooting through her best friend's stuff, as the singer is telling me where to look. Never end up doing the gigs. The money never turns up. And the singer winds up becoming the loan shark's girlfriend so she doesn't get killed. This isn't some crazy underground thing. This is a girl who's got a record deal!"

"Lawrence"

"There was this good-looking, muscley Italian guy named Lawrence that played drums in Toronto. He looked like Rocky. He played with me in a few different bands. Talking to him every day was like reading *Penthouse Forum.* It wasn't just that he picked up a chick. It would be, like, 'I went looking for pants and I walked into this store in the mall and this chick totally gave me the eye. So I grabbed her and she put up the GONE TO LUNCH sign and we're in the back getting it on.' And it was *all true*! At one point, he had a girl that he lived with, and he also used to stay at his mother's place uptown. He'd go there until about midnight, call his live-in girlfriend, and say, 'Yeah, I'm just gonna stay here tonight,' and then he'd go down the street to his ex-girlfriend's place—some chick he was still boning. He slept with her three nights a week, plus his regular girlfriend, plus all these other chicks he was doing at the same time. And it was never, ever enough. As he was telling you a story, he'd see some girl walk by and he'd just be like, *'Ahh, ahhhh.'* At first, you're jealous of the guy and then you realize you're looking at a heroin dick. It's an affliction. He just can't keep up with himself. One time we were in this club that we always played and Lawrence is there with the three-nights-a-week girl. I'm standing at the door, and all of a sudden the seven-days-a-week girl comes walking up the stairs. She's Argentine, about five four, and weighs a hundred pounds soaking wet. But she's like a muscle of fury. She goes, *'WHERE'S LAWRENCE?'* She's wearing these cowboy boots. And she walks up to him, and without taking her eyes off of his eyes, she kicks him in the balls. Then she grabs the other chick by the hair and—bam!—slams the chick's head into her knee. Then she grabs Lawrence by the face and pulls him outside and starts kicking the shit out of him. I later heard the police stopped them, put them both in the car, and took them away."

"Hey, Man, Where's the Snake?"

"I played guitar for a while in this Alice Cooper tribute band called Just Alice. Actually, Jack 'Jackeeboy' Fuller, who played drums for the Brides, played with them, and Lawrence had played with them, too. So I was like, 'Next time someone is leaving on guitar, call me.' As a kid, Alice Cooper was my first ga-ga band. I had all the posters on my bedroom wall. I knew all the music. Just Alice was a real popular tribute band. Nick, the singer, could turn down work, basically. It was weird. We'd travel to gigs and there would be, like, eight phone messages at the bar when we got there and women looking for guys in the band and people screaming. You're thinking, You know, if Alice himself played this bar, it couldn't get much wilder. And the band did the whole Alice stage show. The roadie came out dressed like Frankenstein, swinging the ax. Nick would hang himself onstage. He had the snake. In fact, Alice Cooper had somehow heard about the band and became friends with Nick, and one time Alice had a gig in Toronto and called Nick and asked if he could borrow the snake. I guess Alice's snake was sick or something. Anyway, on gigs, we always brought the snake, which Nick would wrap in a duffel bag and keep in the back of the van. One time, we're loading up our gear, getting ready to drive to a gig. The gig is, like, an hour away, and on the drive there, one of the guys looks in the back and goes, 'Hey, man, where's the snake?' We all turn around and we don't see the snake. So we pull over on the highway, get out and search the van, and there's no snake. Somehow, we got distracted when we were loading the gear and left the snake on the lawn in front of Nick's house. Still in the duffel bag. He had to call this guy and have him go over to the house and then rush us the snake. I mean, what's an Alice Cooper tribute show with no snake, right?"

It had turned into a stiflingly hot summer afternoon on the Cape. The band members paid for breakfast and walked out to their cars; Lee and Rodney Ledbetter got into Lee's Jeep, while the rest of the band climbed into the rented van and I followed in my car. Traffic was bumper-to-bumper. For the next two hours, we slowly made our way off the Cape. I entertained myself by listening to a local classic rock radio station, WKPE "the Rocket." The station was holding a ticket giveaway promotion for the Stones tour. Every few minutes, an announcer came on and advertised the giveaway in the same superenthusiastic basso profundo voice you hear in spots for monster truck rallies: "Classic rock 104.7 the

Rocket is sending two lucky listeners to see the Rolling Stones *rrrr-ock* Fenway! To enter, all you have to do is come to the Rocket's Rolling Stones Rolling Rally. The Rocket will be on the road all over Cape Cod, giving *you* the chance to enter to win tickets to see the Rolling Stones August twenty-first at Fenway. The Rocket's Rolling Stones Rolling Rally—your chance to win tickets from Cape Cod's only *pure* classic rock: 104.7, the *Rrrrr-ocket!*"

The Rolling Rally had touched down at Dino's Sports Bar in Mashpee and Sid's Furniture on Route 28, near the airport. That afternoon, from 2:00 to 4:00 P.M., the Rolling Rally would be at Brewster Wine Cellar & Spirits, in Brewster. "Visit the Rocket crew and enter to win *Rolling Stones tickets!*" the announcer said. I would have liked to stop by, but I was following the Brides to Seekonk, a town close to the venue, where the band was playing that night. Kerry Muldoon had reserved rooms at a cheap roadside motel so the musicians could shower and kill time before the show. (The band planned to drive back to New York City following the gig.) At the motel, I hung out in Lee and Rodney's room, and we vegged and watched a nature show called "Ape to Man." The curtains were partly drawn and rays of soft yellow late-afternoon light streamed in, catching the dust in the air. After a while, Lee and Rodney fell asleep and I channel-surfed. Just after 6:00 P.M., Lee woke up and said, "What time did Moe say we were leaving for the gig? Six-twenty?" At exactly 6:20, there was a knock on the door, and the band gathered in the parking lot to drive to the show.

The concert was at a place called White's of Westport, which I'd noticed on my drive to the Cape the day before because its big lighted sign was visible from the interstate. White's had the aspect of one of those family-style restaurants that for generations has hosted birthday and graduation and retirement parties—only it had expanded over time from something intimate to the size of a car dealership, with reception rooms shooting off a long hallway and, at the far end of the building, almost as an afterthought, the original restaurant.

The Brides were performing in the grand banquet room, a cavernous space with high ceilings, dinner tables for eight, and the sort of low wooden stage common to high school auditoriums. While the band set up their equipment for a sound check, I wandered around the building, peeking into various rooms. In one, the Joseph Case High School class of 1960 was holding its forty-fifth reunion. I asked a woman sitting behind a desk in the hall if White's usually hosted rock bands. "On occasion," she said, "but mostly we do a lot of dinner theater."

Because of the setting, the show that night felt hokey, as if the Brides were a lounge act. An army of waiters dressed in tuxedo outfits rushed around the room filling drink orders as the band played. The audience members didn't strain to involve themselves in the show; they seemed well aware that the actual Stones would be in Boston in a week and therefore treated the Brides as a kind of snack before the main course. Maurice seemed to be aware of this, too, and was visibly agitated all night. He volleyed insults at Mick Jagger again, saying he would "wipe the floor with that motherfucker," and he chastised the band for not playing the way he wanted them to. He appeared to be waging war onstage. He looked miserable.

Earlier, I had been eating in the original White's restaurant when Maurice had come in, sat down, and ordered a bowl of chowder. It was rare that I was alone with Maurice, and on such occasions I was made slightly uncomfortable by his habit of talk-ing *at* a person and getting worked up, then misdirecting his anger or frustration toward whomever he was speaking to. "None of these guys would make it in the real Brides, except maybe Lee," Maurice said in the restaurant. "None of these guys are able to anticipate where the show is going, or where I'm going, and I constantly have to direct them." I suggested that maybe it was be-cause this particular group of musicians had been playing together only a few months. Maurice shook his head in disagreement. "In the old Brides, there was this natural thing where everyone was locked in. Now I've got this booker up in Canada and he's talking to me about getting the old Brides back together to do another tour." I thought the prospect would make him happy, but he shrugged. "The sad truth is the Brides are over," he said, and his tone softened into a melancholy reminiscence. "The real Brides was this incredible ten-year period between 1980 and 1990. But when you're in it, you don't realize that someday it's going to end. You're young and you just don't think about it."

7

On Friday, August 19, a week after the Blushing Brides had played Cape Cod, Sticky Fingers kicked off its own three-day mini-tour of Massachusetts with an engagement at the Half Time Grill, a shoddy-looking bar at the foot of Cape Cod. An hour before the concert, as a fat yellow moon hung low in the sky, Dan Gorgone, Kevin Gleeson, and George Steckert stood in the bar's parking lot, discussing, with some urgency, where they would sleep that night. Glen was spending the weekend in Boston with his new girlfriend, Lisa, and had neglected to arrange accommodations for the band.

"Okay, I say we get in my car and drive to some of those hotels we passed on the way here," Dan said.

"Who's going to pay for the rooms?" George asked, irritated. "Glen already owes me money from the last gig."

"I'll front the room cost and Glen can reimburse me," Dan said helpfully, and then climbed into his Isuzu Trooper.

I hadn't seen the band since the night in Long Island, a month earlier. On the way to find a hotel, Dan and Kevin told me about a recent road trip, during which Sticky Fingers had performed in Las Vegas, then played in front of five thousand people at a town fair in Santa Clarita, California, near Los Angeles. The Las Vegas show coincided with a record heat wave in the city. "We played in one-hundred-and-twenty-degree temperatures, on a metal stage, facing the sun," Dan said, incredulous. "It was like playing inside a microwave oven."

"It was inhuman, man," Kevin rasped from the backseat. He was smoking a cigarette, fully Keithed up, wearing sunglasses, even though it was dark out.

The big news to emerge from the trip was that during the Santa Clarita show, the band had had a run-in with the *other* Sticky Fingers, the group based in Southern California. During the concert a man had approached the stage and handed Glen a folded piece of paper. Glen assumed the man wanted to request a song, but instead was served with a cease-and-desist order, which stated that the other Sticky Fingers owned the trademark to the name in California; under the law, the order stated, it was illegal for Glen's Sticky Fingers to perform anywhere in the state. (This was before the band changed its name to The Hollywood Stones.) "Glen was fuming," Dan said.

The next day, Glen sent Dan to meet with a lawyer in the San Fernando Valley to discuss the document's validity. "The lawyer wanted me to pay a twenty-five-hundred-dollar retainer fee, plus six hundred for the consultation time," Dan said. "He said, 'It was my understanding you were hiring me.' I said, 'Between you and me, I'm just the drummer. Let me tell you what my understanding is: I'm walking out the door and not paying you anything.'" Dan shook his head. "I don't know how those guys can claim they own the right to the name anyway. As I understand it from Glen, this version of Sticky Fingers has been around for twenty-five years, which is a hell of a lot longer than those other guys."

I actually saw the other Sticky Fingers perform one night months later at the Hollywood Palladium on Sunset Boulevard in Los Angeles, and they couldn't have been nicer guys, although they did seem to take a mischievous joy in taunting Glen. The band's singer, a tall, lanky guy who goes by the name Dick Swagger, claimed responsibility for the cease-and-desist order. "I don't understand why he can't get a gig on his side of the country if he's been doing it so long," Dick Swagger said. "I've been going by Sticky Fingers for ten years. I own the service mark in California, so if he *is* going to come over here and use the name Sticky Fingers, he's going to get some legal action from me." (Not long after the California road trip, Glen removed the "Tour Dates" page from the band's Web site so as to shroud his engagements from the other Sticky Fingers.)

As Dan, Kevin, and I were driving along, Dan spotted a motel off the main highway. A sign out front said VACANCY and $55 A NIGHT. He pulled into the parking lot and everyone got out of the car and walked into the motel office. That weekend, Dan had a guest along, a high-strung woman named Donnell, who sang in a Blondie tribute band he'd recently put together on the side, even though she was a brunette; evidently, she had accompanied the band on the last few road trips as a backup vocalist. Dan rang the desk bell. After a moment, a desk clerk, a guy in his early twenties, came out from behind a curtain.

"How much are the rooms?" Dan said.

"Eighty-five dollars a night," the desk clerk said.

Dan looked confused. "Any deal you can make?" he asked. "We're a working band, playing a show in the area. Frankly, we can't afford eighty-five dollars a night. We stopped because your sign said fifty-five dollars."

"That's on weekdays," the clerk said.

"Well," Dan said, "can you meet us somewhere in the middle?"

The clerk thought for a moment and said he could do seventy-five dollars. The total, after tax, came to $82.50. Dan seemed pleased with the deal he'd negotiated. He turned to Donnell and, in a worldly tone, said, "This is life on the road, D."

When we got back to the Half Time Grill, Glen was on a stone patio out back, talking happily with some friends he knew from his days living in New England, most of them relatives of the late Bobby Chouinard, the wildman drummer who'd performed with Sticky Fingers. One of the people in the group was Bobby's nephew, Roger Chouinard, who was a promoter and had set up the Half Time Grill show. "I used to visit your uncle's grave and take a bottle of Jack Daniel's," Glen said to Roger, who nodded solemnly.

Glen motioned to another man in the group and said to me, "That guy is good friends with the chief of security for the Stones." He seemed to be speaking loudly so as to be overheard by his new girlfriend, Lisa, who was standing nearby. Lisa was the British woman he'd met in Florida. Since they'd begun dating, Glen had embarked on an exercise regimen and had curbed his drinking (at the moment, he was sipping bottled water). Lisa was deeply tanned, about forty, with dyed blond hair and a chesty build.

"On Sunday, he's going to get us into the Stones after-party," Glen continued loudly, pointing to the man with the Stones connection. "At the Four Seasons."

The Half Time Grill was spread over two rooms and separated by a hallway. In the back room was a pool table and a dartboard; in the front was a bar, a jukebox, a plywood stage barely big enough to fit the five band members, and a half-dozen TV sets, all tuned to a Red Sox game. There was no dressing area, so when it was time for Sticky Fingers to perform, the musicians took turns slipping into a little office to change into their stage outfits. That weekend, the band was playing with the latest in a line of bassists, a guy from Long Island who called himself "Jazzkat." Jazzkat spent several months with the band and never ceased to appear deeply strange. He was in his forties, bald and wiry, with skeletal features and an unhealthy pallor. He talked a lot about "vibes," claimed associations with numerous famous musicians, and insisted on his own hotel room on road trips for health reasons that remained vague and ominous. He died the following summer.

The bar was running a promotion that night tied to the Stones tour; anyone who ordered a drink made with Effen brand vodka was entered into a raffle to win tickets to opening night at Fenway Park. The contest offered better than fair odds, I thought, considering there were only thirty or so people in the bar. As

Glen was about to take the stage, he looked dispiritedly at the half-empty room and said, "I should be so drunk right now."

The show wasn't that bad, although, to be honest, having traveled around with Sticky Fingers and the Blushing Brides for months, I'd heard the Stones' greatest hits so many times the songs had begun to lose all luster. I dreaded it whenever one of the bands began a long number like "Midnight Rambler"; that the musicians never seemed to tire of the songs I found remarkable. There wasn't any reason for Sticky Fingers to give it their all at the Half Time Grill anyway. Competing with a televised Red Sox game in New England when the team is in the middle of a pennant race is the definition of show business futility. The only person whose eyes never left the stage was Lisa. It was her first time seeing Glen perform and she stood in the center of the room, smiling adoringly. Glen responded, in turn, with a showy display of classic lead singer moves: he mussed his shaggy hair; he gyrated his bony hips; he rested his arm on Kevin's shoulder the way lead singers do with their lead guitarists. When the band played "Start Me Up" and the song came to the part of the lyric that goes "you make a grown man *cryyy*," Glen sang the line to Lisa, as if he'd written the words himself, especially for her.

The next day, we had some time to kill because the band wasn't due in Worcester until later that evening. Kevin and Dan and Donnell drove to Plymouth Rock to sightsee, while George and I drove in my car to Providence to visit some record stores I knew about there. Earlier, at the hotel, everyone had been sitting around on a deck drinking coffee when Donnell began complaining about an acid-reflux condition that was acting up. "I need to get some milk," she kept saying. Now, in the car, George said disgustedly, "Why would you bring a chick on the road? It puts a crimp in the whole weekend." He furrowed his brow. "This is the third straight gig she's been on. A few weeks ago, we played in Maryland and I met this hot girl in the audience"—I gave George a knowing look—"yeah, it was great, man. Except we had to leave right after the gig because Donnell had to get back to New York to go to some acting audition." George seemed to envision another missed opportunity this weekend, and furrowed his brow again. "If she gets paid," he said, "I'm going to be *pissed*."

George had been in low spirits since the weekend began, owing partly to the fact that Glen hadn't yet paid him for a wedding gig the band had played a week earlier. George was normally broke, but without the money he earned in Sticky Fingers he was hopelessly so. Also, Glen had lately been threatening to fire George if he didn't cut his hair, which Glen deemed to have grown beyond Ron Wood length. "With Glen, you never know when it's going to be your last gig," George said resignedly.

Just outside Providence, the rock station we were listening to played a minor classic by the Stones called "Shine a Light"—a soulful tune with rich gospel piano chords and a sweeping chorus that goes:

> *May the good Lord shine a light on you,*
> *Make every song you sing your favorite tune.*
> *May the good Lord shine a light on you,*
> *Warm like the evening sun.*

George cranked up the volume and I found myself driving faster down the highway, the way you do when you're behind the wheel and under the spell of a good song. George laughed, suddenly in good spirits again, and said, "If you ain't feeling this, you don't have a *pulse!*"

In 1981, the Stones spent several weeks rehearsing for their world tour at a secluded recording studio on a dairy farm in North Brookfield, Massachusetts. By then, the Stones had outlasted the Beatles and Led Zeppelin and the '81 tour solidified forever their transition from a big rock band to the *biggest rock band in the world*—an attendance-record-setting, corporate-sponsored, global monolith. According to a not-so-presciently titled book about the tour, *The Last Tour,* by Peter Goddard, at a concert in New Orleans that year the band played in front of 87,000 people at the Superdome. When it was announced the Stones would perform five nights in the New York City area, four million fans vied for the one hundred thousand tickets. During outdoor shows, Mick Jagger hovered above crowds in the kind of cherry picker ladder used by firemen to rescue people from twenty-story buildings. Goddard described the near-soulless homogeneity of seeing the Stones in concert that summer: "Movement is almost an illusion on the tour," he wrote. "It gives the appearance of change where there is, in fact, little change. They'll play in nearly identical concrete football stadiums throughout the country in nearly identical suburbs to nearly identical white, middle-class audiences, who'll respond at nearly identical points in the show. Denver might just as well be Detroit. Mick says when a tour's all over, he forgets it completely. No wonder."

But before the tour started, the Stones played an unannounced warm-up concert at Sir Morgan's Cove, a small rock club in Worcester, Massachusetts, that has since been renamed the Lucky Dog Music Hall. It was the band's first live performance in more than three years, and when word of the concert leaked, four thousand fans showed up and stood out in the rain or on the hoods of cars or on the rooftops of nearby buildings, hoping to catch sight of the band. On a wall inside the Lucky Dog is a framed plaque to commemorate the night the Stones played there. The plaque reads: "On Monday, September 14, 1981, play-ing under the name 'The Cockroaches,' the biggest band in the world kicked off what would be the biggest tour of the year, in this room, on this stage." The Lucky Dog is one of those hole-in-the-wall rock clubs with all the size and charm of a one-car garage. To see the biggest rock band in the world in a room that small would have been a rare and singular experience.

The club is still located in the same spot, in a three-story building on a weedy block of downtown Worcester. George and I arrived in the late afternoon, and Dan and Kevin soon pulled up. Kevin got out and pointed up at the club's marquee, grinning. That night, in big letters, the marquee said SAT AUG 20 ROLLING STONES TRIBUTE STICKY FINGERS. Below that it read FRI SEPT 16 DIZZY REED OF GUNS N' ROSES. The show was a few hours away, but no one had heard from Glen all day. Dan pulled a cell phone from a belt holster and dialed. He was dressed like a dad on a fam-ily vacation: denim shorts, a loose-fitting muscle shirt, sneakers with white socks pulled to the calf, and a fanny pack around his waist. "How far outside of town?" I heard him say into the phone. "And how much a night? . . . Okay." Dan hung up and said, "Jazzkat says there's a Best Western a few miles outside of town with rooms available." We all drove to the hotel and booked rooms. Dan dropped his bags and said, "I'm headed to the pool";

and Glen finally called to tell the guys to be back at the Lucky Dog by 9:00 P.M.; and Donnell complained again about her acid reflux; and George took a nap and pretended she wasn't there. Then everyone drove back to the Lucky Dog.

In the basement dressing room before the show, there was a sense of occasion, born from the knowledge that Sticky Fingers would be playing on the same stage as the Stones. Everyone was smoking cigarettes and talking over one another, and Glen was back to drinking whiskey instead of water. He had brought his girlfriend, Lisa, again, and she sat coolly dragging on a smoke, dressed in tight jeans and a blue silk blouse that was fastened at the breast with a brooch. As it happened, it was a stage outfit; that night, she was making her debut as the band's new backup singer. As conversations swirled above them, George knelt down and patiently taught Lisa backing vocal parts to Stones hits. "Okay," George said. " 'Jumpin' Jack Flash.' *It's aaalll riiiiight now.* Roll it. Do that sister thing. . . . 'Satisfaction.' *I can't get no!* It's pretty much just shouts. . . . 'Miss You.' Get breathy. *Ah-Ah. Ah-Ah. Ah-Ah. Ahhhh.*"

George seemed struck by something, stopped his lesson, and looked up at Glen. "I love Jagger, man," he said. "Every flow of music that came by, he adapted and made it so cool. 'Miss You'— that's a disco tune."

Glen nodded in agreement. "When people were doing disco and everyone hated it, the Stones went out and said, 'All right. You want to hear disco? This is how you do.' " A cigarette dangling between his lips, Glen began stomping out the beat to "Miss You" on the floor with his foot. "It's that beat," Glen said, stomping.

Because the Stones were kicking off a world tour that weekend, I assumed the Lucky Dog would be packed: everyone who couldn't get tickets would want to see Sticky Fingers, and the people who *had* tickets would want to see Sticky Fingers anyway to psych themselves up for the Stones. But the crowd wasn't much bigger than it had been the night before at the Half Time Grill—maybe forty people. The room was dark, except for the stage lights, which cast a red-and-green glow on the empty dance floor. When Sticky Fingers finally took the stage, a handful of people wandered out to dance. Most everyone was wearing some kind of slogan T-shirt, and as Kevin kicked off the show with "Happy," I read the slogans, which seemed to match up well to each person's appearance. One guy with frosted hair and a soul patch was wearing a T-shirt that said UNDERNEATH THIS SHIRT I'M NAKED. A middle-aged guy with shaggy gray hair wore a Yard-birds concert tee. A hippie with thinning blond hair had on a T-shirt from the Gathering of the Vibes jam-band festival. A tough-looking guy wore a Harley-Davidson T-shirt. When the band played "Sympathy for the Devil," Glen jumped down from the stage and dirty-danced with a woman in the crowd, a petite brunette with real spunk in her step. Her T-shirt said MORE COW-BELL.

The final engagement of the weekend was on Sunday afternoon, at the house of a Stones fan named Ritchie, who was throwing a bash for his friends before they all went to see the Stones later that night. Ritchie lived sixty miles east of Worcester, near Boston, and on the drive there George and I listened to the local radio DJs as they talked about how great it was that the Stones were back in town and what a historic night of rock and roll it promised to be and how they were cueing up "ten in a row on a Stones weekend." George didn't have a ticket and didn't have enough money to pay a scalper, but he was hoping to finagle his way into the concert somehow. I'd bought a ticket for $200 on eBay, the most money I'd ever spent to see a concert.

Ritchie's house was in a wooded suburb north of Boston, on a hilly plot of land that managed to contain, within an acre or so, an in-ground pool, a pool house, a tennis court, a putting green, and a running waterfall display. Ritchie, who was compactly built and Italian, ran a car service firm called Satisfaction Transportation. That day, he wore a T-shirt imprinted on the front with a picture of Keith Richards.

I asked him how he had come to hire Sticky Fingers.

"It was between these guys and the Blushing Brides," he said, taking a drag of his cigarette. "They're the two best around. Everyone else—Hot Rocks and those other bands—are shit." Ritchie turned to face a beefy-looking guy standing nearby. "Hey, will you go up and make sure the house is locked?" he said. "I don't want people in the house during the party." He looked back to me and said, "Like I said, it was between these guys and the Blushing Brides, and the Blushing Brides weren't available." Ritchie recalled going to Boston to see the Brides at the Channel. "This was between eighty-one and eighty-nine, when people weren't sure if the Stones were going to stay together," he said. "The Blushing Brides had a *big* following. Three thousand people would show up. I used to wait on line to see the Blushing Brides."

For the party, Ritchie had gone all out: caterers were stationed by the pool house, serving shrimp and beef tips, and guests were given specially made T-shirts printed with the words STICKY FINGERS AUGUST 21 2005. I met one couple who'd come all the way from Arizona, and I saw Gary Cherone from the band Extreme hanging out near the stage that had been set up on the tennis court. Mostly, I sat with Kevin and George at a courtside table. That day happened to be Kevin's forty-sixth birthday. "I share it with Count Basie and Kenny Rogers, the gambla," Kevin said, leaning back in his chair, eyes closed, sunning his skinny chest.

After a while, George got up and walked down to the pool house to load up on shrimp and beef tips. Soon after, Glen arrived with Lisa, stopping to socialize with Ritchie and his wife before joining the rest of the band at the table. He wore a black dress shirt and designer sunglasses and sipped from a bottle of Southern Comfort. At one point, Glen looked curiously at the ground where George had been sitting. Reaching down, he picked up a crushed-out cigarette butt, and, inspecting the evidence, said, "Winston 100." He looked disgusted. "That's some white-trash shit—grinding out your cigarette on the host's property," Glen said. "It better not belong to George. I'll tell you something else. That boy better cut his hair, or he's out in a few more gigs. I know plenty of guys who can do the Ron Wood like Kevin does the Keith and I do the Mick." As if to illustrate the point, Glen rose from his chair and asked Kevin to walk with him down to the pool, where the party was centered. Almost immediately, a crowd swelled around them, as if Mick and Keith had appeared in the flesh. Women lined up to have their pictures taken and men looked at one another and exchanged an amused look, as if to say, Do you believe these two? I overheard one woman say to her friend, "I can't get over it. He looks so much like Keith!"

Glen and Kevin basked in the attention, smiling and posing for pictures. In his best Cockney accent, Glen introduced himself to one of the women: " 'Ello, luv."

I didn't actually get to see Sticky Fingers perform that afternoon, because soon after Glen arrived I drove to Boston to attend another party—this one thrown by the group of Stones superfans who call themselves the Shidoobees.

I'd heard about the Shidoobees because they sometimes hired Sticky Fingers or the Blushing Brides to perform at their annual get-togethers, and also because Kerry Muldoon, the Brides' manager, was friendly with the head Shidoobee, a fifty-something guy from Annapolis, Maryland, who went by the name Stonesdoug. I'd spoken with Stonesdoug on the phone a few days before the party and he'd said that because it was opening night of the tour, Shidoobees from as far away as Japan were coming.

The party was being held at an Irish bar a few blocks from Fenway Park. When I arrived, about two hundred people, baby boomers in the main, were stuffed into the bar's narrow basement, drinking and singing along to Stones songs blasting from the sound system. Many were wearing lime green T-shirts printed with the words SHIDOOBEE CREW 2005–06. Each time a song came on, everyone erupted with surprise, as if they hadn't heard that old hit a thousand times before.

Eventually, I found Stonesdoug standing in the back of the bar, holding court. He had silvery hair and a beatific grin on his reddened face, as if he were in the midst of a religious experience. "Opening night!" Stonesdoug shouted above the noise. "It's always exciting." The last time the Stones had toured, in 2003, Stonesdoug went to thirty-five shows, including three in Sweden. The first time he saw the Stones, at the Steel Pier in Atlantic City in 1966, he was fifteen and Brian Jones was still in the band. As the Stones drove away, Stonesdoug tried to grab the buttons off Brian Jones's blazer. "I get into a trance when I go to a show," Stonesdoug told me. In 2000, he started an Internet chat room for Stones fans called Shidoobee with Stonesdoug (*Shidoobee* comes from a line in "Shattered"). Mostly, the Shidoobees socialize on-line, but once a year they throw a party in Wildwood, New Jersey, and when the Stones tour, they go into high gear, organizing gatherings in each city where the band performs. One Shidoobee I spoke to told me the group is an enabler. "You end up going to way more shows than you would normally," he said. "People say, 'You've already seen them once.' Well, you had sex once. But you're going to have it again. It could be better the next time."

I squeezed into a booth with a couple of Shidoobees who had traveled from Sweden, and one from Finland. The Finn pointed to his friends and, over the noise, yelled, "We have a long, dedicated worshiping of the Rolling Stones!" Some time later I went outside to take a phone call from George, who had called to tell me that some guy at Ritchie's party had given him a Stones ticket, so he'd lucked his way into the concert after all. When I went back into the bar, a Shidoobee named Shirley was cutting a birthday cake with tongue-and-lips icing, and everyone was singing along to "Under My Thumb." Shirley's husband watched with wry amusement. "I'm not a Shidoobee," he told me, explaining that he belonged to an Internet group called

Backstreets that was devoted to Bruce Springsteen. "We talk pol-
itics and get involved in charities," he said. "One of the members'
sons is stationed in Iraq."

Stonesdoug gathered his flock, and soon everyone marched
outside and walked over to the stadium. As we got closer, the
streets began to resemble a parade: traffic cops were blowing
whistles and waving their hands wildly at passing cars, and groups
of Stones fans clogged the sidewalks. In front of the stadium, the
air was smoky from food vendors grilling hamburgers and hot
sausages, and merchandise booths were doing a brisk business selling Stones T-shirts printed with *both* the tongue-and-lips logo
and the Red Sox insignia. Scalpers weaved through the crowd,
holding tickets. As part of his gubernatorial campaign, Arnold
Schwarzenegger was using the concert as a fund-raising event (in
exchange for a $100,000 contribution, you could watch the Stones
with the Terminator), and demonstrators from the California
Nurses Association held picket signs that said STOP ARNOLD. I stood
outside for a minute, taking in the swirl of Stones fans, the smell
of the grilling meat, the noise, the TV news crews, the scalpers.
Then I said good-bye to Stonesdoug and the other Shidoobees
and joined the stream of people heading into the stadium.

At the press conference the Stones held at Lincoln Center three
months earlier, the details of the Bigger Bang tour were announced. The tour was characteristically ambitious: as the Stones
have become older and less of a cultural and artistic force, they
have responded, paradoxically, by doing everything on an out-
sized scale, in the style of a restaurant compensating for average
food by serving large portions. In 1994, the Voodoo Lounge tour

grossed $320 million, then a record amount; the band's 2002–3 Forty Licks tour played to 3.4 million people. The new studio album, *A Bigger Bang,* was being touted as the "longest album since *Exile on Main Street* in 1972." As for the Bigger Bang tour, the first leg was to include thirty-five dates in the United States and Canada (the number would increase to forty-two), before swinging through South America, Japan, and Europe. In addition, the band would be performing on what was being called the biggest, most expensive stage ever built for a rock concert. According to an article in the *Hartford Courant,* the stage was 90 feet high and 280 feet wide, took four days to assemble and thirty hours to tear down, and was moved from city to city on 127 trucks. The most outsize aspect of the tour were the ticket prices, which had ballooned to $450 at the top end (the cheap seats were $64.50). A minimum-wage worker would have to spend two weeks' earnings to get a good seat to see the Stones. Stonesdoug had even scaled back his itinerary this tour—to a mere thirteen shows.

The face value of the ticket I'd bought on eBay was $163, which placed me in roof 7, row B, seat 8—a technical way of saying I was sitting in the nosebleeds, *literally* on the roof of Fenway Park. Had my seat been any higher, I might well have been in the flight path of the planes taking off from Logan Airport. I did, however, have an unobstructed, if long-distance, view of the stage set, which was, in fact, gigantic. It hovered in deep center field like a mothership. The actual stage—the floor where Mick Jagger would soon be strutting—had the dimensions of a basketball court; rising behind it was a massive JumboTron—a TV screen built for a race of giants (or fans seated in section roof 7). On each side of the screen was a four-tier titanium-colored tower that vaguely resembled a casino parking garage; each level contained columns of speakers and room for a few dozen fans, who, through a random lottery, had won the right to (technically) be onstage with the Stones.

When I found my seat, the opening act, the Black Eyed Peas, was already onstage, playing to a half-empty stadium of other people finding their seats. They tried gamely to win the crowd but soon began to yell boosterish things like "Are you ready for the Rolling Stones, Boston?" before scampering off. The next hour passed with the usual preconcert rituals: the grandstands and the grassy outfield filled with pumped-up fans (36,000 in all); innocuous background music was piped through the stadium; and each time the music died down, the crowd screamed for the Stones, who, in the grand showbiz tradition, kept them waiting. Meanwhile, the celebrity attendees milled around in the VIP area near the Red Sox dugout. At one point, there was a commotion and a popping of flashbulbs and Steven Tyler appeared wearing a three-quarter-length snakeskin coat, did a quick turn around the infield, and was gone. Another twenty minutes went by. Finally, at 8:21 P.M., the houselights went dark. Cameras flashed. Zippos flickered. The crowd screamed. Then the JumboTron lit up and a kind of movie trailer appeared—a deep-space montage showing the disembodied heads of the four Stones floating through the cosmos. Then a burst of light, and the real, non-disembodied Mick, Keith, Ronnie, and Charlie, and— "Start me up. If you start me up I'll never stop . . ."

From my seat, the band members appeared impossibly tiny, like figurines atop an elaborately decorated cake, and I fixed my eyes on the JumboTron screen to render them large-scale again. Periodically, I would glance at the stage to remind myself that I wasn't watching the concert on television somewhere—that I was there, in Fenway Park, on opening night. Mick Jagger came out dressed in a fedora and satiny blue pants, doing his Jagger strut, and Keith Richards stalked the stage with his guitar swinging on his shoulder, looking as he always does, both ancient and ageless. The band sounded crisp and well rehearsed, and they played a mix of old hits ("Tumbling Dice," "Satisfaction") and album cuts ("She's So Cold," "Out of Control"), along with a few numbers from the new record so no one could call the concert an oldies show. It was everything you would want from a stadium rock concert: there were pyrotechnics, costume changes, a fifty-foot-tall inflatable tongue, and a stage that moved on a track out into the audience. The tickets may have been expensive, but the Stones worked for their money, dancing and prancing, posing and posturing, singing and playing with abandon for two hours. As the night went on, though, something strange happened: I'd spent so much time with the tribute bands that I began to see the Stones not as originators but as imitators. I noticed how the Stones opened the concert with "Start Me Up," just as Sticky Fingers does, and how Mick Jagger employed Maurice Raymond's trick of mentioning the hometown sports team to curry favor with the crowd. And wasn't the femme hand wave Jagger did right there just like the one Glen did onstage two nights earlier at the Half Time Grill? My reaction was surprising to me, and completely backward, of course, but also understandable. Seeing the Stones in concert is like seeing an expensively produced, elaborately staged, carefully orchestrated tribute show because it is more about memory conjuring than making new memories, about the past rather than the present. As Peter Goddard suggested twenty-four years earlier, the audience knows what will happen before the band even takes the stage. Halfway through the concert, Mick Jagger introduced the band. When he said Keith Richards's name, Richards strode to the microphone in his typical shrug-shouldered style, as if he'd been loading up at the deli tray backstage when someone handed him a guitar and pushed him onstage. The audience, recognizing this familiar ritual, played its part, affectionately yelling, *"Keith! Keith!"* As Richards mumbled his way through his mini-set, people sitting near me began to get up and stretch or sneak off to the bathroom—just like the audience did when Kevin Gleeson of Sticky Fingers sang his Keith set.

8

When the Stones tour came to New York City the following month, I made plans to go to the concert at Madison Square Garden. For the Stones, playing the eighteen-thousand-seat Garden is like playing a club date, and I hoped seeing them in the relative coziness of an arena would be more stirring than opening night at Fenway Park had been. Also, I wanted to see the Stones with a fan, so I bought two tickets and invited Kevin Gleeson. Of all the tribute musicians I'd met, Kevin was the one most devoted to the Stones. I often had the sense that his repertoire on guitar did not extend far beyond Stones songs or the old blues numbers on which they are based. And he seemed to view his life in relation to the Stones, and to Keith Richards in particular, as if Richards was the sun and he was a trailing shadow. Once, we happened to be talking about the Stones' album *Dirty Work,* and Kevin said,

"On *Dirty Work,* first thing I hear is 'Sleep Tonight' and Keith being honest. When Keith sang 'Sleep Tonight,' I was going through the same thing, coming back from drug addiction, just wanted to get some sleep tonight. A new Stones album would come out and I'd take the music and apply it to my own existence." Even in casual conversation, his thoughts had a way of returning to the Stones, like a record needle that slips into a familiar groove. His stories about the band carried the vivid detail of an eyewitness. One day while we were driving to a Sticky Fingers show, the subject of Richards's famous Toronto drug bust came up and Kevin said, somewhat dramatically, "I can set the scene. The Royal Canadian Mounties are at the hotel. They bust Keith for trafficking and possession. Mick is afraid the Mounties will bust the whole band. Keith starts going through withdrawal on the bathroom floor. Bill Wyman walks in and finds Keith in the fetal position, in tears. It's the only recorded time anyone has ever said they've seen Keith crying."

Of course, Kevin had never met any of the Stones, and the closest he would likely come to doing so was being in the same arena or stadium. Some tribute performers *have* met the famous musicians they are pretending to be. For instance, the members of Dark Star Orchestra have been joined onstage twice by Bob Weir, and the Eddie Van Halen in the Atomic Punks once spent a night riding around Hollywood with the real Eddie Van Halen as Eddie played rough mixes from the *Balance* album. For tribute performers it can be a surreal experience to find themselves standing alongside the person they have spent years idolizing and imitating. Frankie Italiano, who plays bass in Maiden NY, an Iron Maiden tribute, once told me about the friendship that has developed between him and Iron Maiden's founding bassist, Steve Harris.

Frankie said, "I got a call one day: ' 'Ello, mate. This is Steve.' I'm like, 'Steve who?' 'It's Steve Harris, mate.' He was with my friend Joe, who was the drum tech for Anthrax for ten years and knows all these guys through touring. Joe told him I was a fan. He said, 'I hear you play tennis. We'll have to have a hit sometime.' Iron Maiden was performing in L.A., and Joe and I were planning on flying out there to see them anyway, so I told Steve we should play a game in Los Angeles. He's like, 'Okay, mate. Let's do it then.' Iron Maiden was playing the Universal Amphitheatre. We got to go backstage, and it was a total scene. Gene Simmons was there. Alec Baldwin was there with his family. I'm thinking, Holy shit, *this is Steve Harris from Iron Maiden!* If my friends from the tribute band were here, they'd freak." The following day, Frankie and Steve Harris met to play tennis at the Beverly Hills Country Club. "I've got to tell you about the wristbands," Frankie continued. "So we're playing tennis and I'm still freaked out about the guy, 'cause he's *fucking Steve Harris.* So anyway, onstage he always wears wristbands the same colors as the West Ham soccer club, his favorite team. I'm thinking, If I can just get a pair of those wristbands for my tribute band, I'm set. We're playing tennis and at one point he opens up his gym bag and he says, 'Hey, mate, you need a wristband?' "

Not all encounters between a tribute performer and the real rock star turn out so happily. I once met the singer of a Mötley Crüe tribute who got into a physical altercation with Vince Neil. Neil had been going from city to city judging bikini contests to promote a line of swimwear and thought it would be fun to perform with a tribute band. "We met him before the show and he was a nice guy," the tribute singer told me. "Then he gets onstage and he's drunk and disoriented. I'm singing the words and he's singing some gibberish like, 'She's a cool, cool cat.' So I stopped passing him the mike. He didn't like that. He looked at me and gave me a good old shove—right into the drum riser."

But the Stones exist on a rarefied level of rock stardom. The band members travel by private jet and are led to and from concerts by a police escort; they don't do record store signings, or radio call-in shows, or fan meet-and-greets. When they grant interviews, it is selectively and, one senses, out of career necessity. There may have been a time when the Stones were accessible to their fans, but it has long since passed. In all of his years in Sticky Fingers, Glen Carroll has never met any of the Stones (his entrée to the after-party on the opening night of the tour in Boston never panned out), and the only time the Stones ever acknowledged the existence of the Blushing Brides was Mick Jagger's dismissive comment in the *Boston Globe*. After considerable effort, Stonesdoug has managed to exchange a word or two with Keith, Ronnie, and Charlie, and on the Bigger Bang tour he would be invited backstage by Chuck Leavell, the touring keyboard player. But even a backstage pass doesn't guarantee contact with the Stones themselves; each of the band members is rumored to have their own dressing room, a backstage to the backstage, out of reach of record company publicity men and radio contest winners and superfans like Stonesdoug. When I began work on this book, I had hoped to interview the Stones—to ask them what they thought of tribute bands like Sticky Fingers, and whether they were flattered or irritated by someone like Glen earning a living singing their songs. I contacted the band's publicist explaining that I was writing a book about tribute bands and sought permission to hang out behind the scenes at a concert in order to compare the real and the ersatz versions. I received this brief reply: "It sounds like a wonderful concept but the Stones will not be available."

An hour before the Stones concert, I met Kevin in front of Madison Square Garden. That day, he was dressed in blue jeans, sneakers, and a T-shirt. I hardly recognized him. Out of his Keith costume, he appeared deflated, like a superhero in civilian dress. I noticed for the first time that his tangled hair was going gray and receding.

As it happened, the Shidoobees were holding a get-together at a bar on Eighth Avenue, a few blocks from the Garden. We stopped by before the show because I'd arranged to buy two tickets from one of the Shidoobees. The bar was dimly lit, noisy, and packed with Stones fans. I ordered a beer and asked Kevin how he was doing. "I'm strung out from the road," he said wearily but not unhappily, and explained that he'd just returned from a whirlwind road trip with Sticky Fingers. It took place over a long weekend and began with a drive to a college in North Carolina, followed by a nine-hour drive to another college, this time in Tuscaloosa, Alabama. From Tuscaloosa, the band drove to Atlanta, parked Dan's car at the airport, flew to Lake Tahoe to play a wedding reception, flew back to Atlanta the next day, picked up Dan's car, and drove fourteen hours back to New York. Kevin returned home at 5:00 A.M. on Monday morning, just in time to drop off his guitars, change, and head to his job at the police department.

I asked him how the shows had rated musically, and he said, a little glumly, "Okay, I guess. Glen has been drinking heavy again." Kevin said that the band had played a private party in Boulder,

Colorado, and the host had taken exception. "He came up afterwards and told us, 'I know the Stones are legendary for their partying, but I think you guys took it too far.' "

I thought Kevin would enjoy being around other Stones fans, but he seemed weirded out by the Shidoobees and uncomfortable in a bar. When the guy with the tickets showed up, I paid him $150 for the pair and we walked back to Madison Square Garden. A crowd was gathered outside the arena, including a number of middle-aged fathers taking their sons to see the Stones. A pretty TV newswoman was interviewing one of the boys, who looked about ten. "Why do you want to see the Rolling Stones?" she asked.

" 'Cause they're cool," the boy said.

The newswoman gave a winking smile to the camera and, turning back to the boy, said, "But they're older than your parents."

The boy shrugged, not yet at the age where that was damning.

Inside the arena, a woman stood at the top of a short flight of stairs, directing concertgoers. We waited in line, and then a security guard patted us down and another uniformed guy scanned our tickets and said, "All the way to the top." As we ascended several escalators and a final flight of stairs, I realized with growing dismay that our seats were high above stage left, in the very last row of the arena. In front of us, a ceiling beam jutted down partway, so that anytime we rose to our feet we had to crouch to see the stage. The guy sitting next to me was holding a pair of binoculars.

Alanis Morissette was the opening act. She came out onstage wearing baggy cargo pants and a formless black shirt. Kevin turned to me and said, "I thought she'd come out with a nice dress on or something. Geez. She looks like Steve Marriott from Humble Pie." Alanis played a brief set of her hits and then exited. The houselights came on, suffusing the Garden with that warm, hazy, yellow half-light particular to arena rock concerts.

The building buzzed with preconcert activity: people were searching for their seats or getting up to buy beer or walking down to get a closer look at the stage before returning to their faraway corner of the arena. At one point, a miniature blimp appeared and circled around the arena; printed on its side was an ad for Ameriquest Mortgage Company, the corporation sponsoring the tour. I'd never heard Kevin say a bad word about the Stones, but at the sight of the blimp he said, "That ain't too rock and roll. I'm surprised they're not dropping mortgage applications on the seats."

As we waited for the Stones to go on, the man sitting to my left, the one holding binoculars, struck up a conversation. "First time seeing the Stones?" he asked in a British accent. He introduced himself as Roy and explained that he had flown from England especially to see the Stones at Madison Square Garden. He was in his fifties, with a high-banged bowl haircut and a look of happy anticipation on his face, like a child about to receive a present. "I've seen 'em on ev'ry tour since eighty-one," he said.

Kevin, sitting to my right, leaned over and said to Roy, "I saw them here at the Garden in seventy-five."

"I can do better than that," Roy said good-naturedly. "I saw them in sixty-six at a theater in London with Brian Jones. Great show."

It turned out that Roy had seen the Stones dozens of times all over the world—in Paris, in Knebworth, England, at New

York's Shea Stadium. He was sitting alone, prompting me to ask if he was married.

"Of course not," he said. "I couldn't go to all these Stones shows if I was married. I flew over here with some friends. They have seats down on the floor, a few rows from the stage."

Kevin asked Roy if he had seen the Counterfeit Stones, a popular Rolling Stones tribute band in Britain.

"I've seen the Counterfeit Stones many times," Roy said. "In fact, there was a quote in a British paper from Jerry Hall, who said they're better than the Stones." Roy chuckled. "Jerry would say something like that. Ol' Jerry."

I waited for Kevin to tell Roy that he was Keith in a tribute band, but he didn't. Instead, he was mostly quiet and appeared almost contemptuous of Roy's dedication to the Stones; later, when Roy went to the concession stand, Kevin said to me, "Flying halfway across the world to see a Stones show? That's crazy."

At one point, Roy got on the subject of how the Stones are viewed in England. "They slag the Stones something terrible," Roy said. "They can't get over their age."

Americans seemed focused on the topic, too. Mick Jagger was sixty-two when the tour began; Keith Richards was sixty-one; Charlie Watts was sixty-four and in remission from cancer; and Ronnie Wood was fifty-eight. Collectively, the Stones were 245. Practically every newspaper article about the Bigger Bang tour highlighted the band members' ages, or the fact that the Stones had been touring since the Kennedy administration, and concert reviewers grappled with the seldom-posed question of whether senior citizens could still "rock." The reviewers generally fell into two camps of critical opinion: the Stones were boldly defying old age (GRANDDADS OF ROCK STILL HAVE IT GOING ON—

Seattle Times) or they were geezers making one last stand (STONES BREAK RECORDS AND HIPS IN WHAT FEELS LIKE THEIR FINAL FLING— *New York Post*). There was great concern among fans like Roy and Kevin that, given the Stones' advanced ages and recent health problems, this would be the band's last large-scale tour. "Have you seen pictures of Keith's hands?" Kevin once said to me. "There's so much talk about how his guitar playing has degraded, and I can see why. Every joint is blown up like a balloon. You know, the little jewels we get from Keith today are when he does his ballads. He'll surprise you—and it touches your heart. You got to admire the old dog." Speculation about this being the band's last go-round increased significantly when, halfway through the tour, Keith Richards fell out of a palm tree in Fiji and underwent emergency cranial surgery. Richards's simian likeness, which has only increased with age, seemed more pronounced than ever with the news that he'd been foraging for coconuts.

Just shy of ten o'clock, the lights darkened and an expectant hush swept across the arena. I had trouble seeing anything in the dark, but Roy exclaimed, "I see Ronnie!" and soon my eyes adjusted and I could see skinny men standing beside tall stacks of amplifiers. We watched Keith Richards strap on his Telecaster and Mick Jagger stride coolly to the microphone. Jagger was wearing one of his characteristically flashy outfits, the centerpiece of which was a black sequined half shirt that exposed his muscled belly. In reviews of the tour, much would be made of Jagger's prime physical condition given his age, and watching him perform I had to agree, although I'm unsure if wearing a belly shirt at sixty-two is something to aspire to.

Suddenly, the familiar riff of "Start Me Up" rang out from Richards's guitar, kicking off the concert. Kevin raised his voice to be heard over the music, and said, "We'll hear plenty of riffs tonight; we're here to see the riff master." Then, with a look of deep contentment, he added, "This is like church for me."

The concert followed the same course as it had on opening night in Boston—as it would throughout the tour. After having seen only one show, I knew the basic outline of the evening before it began. The Stones would play a mix of hits, a cover or two (in this case Bob Marley's "Get Up, Stand Up"), and a few new songs. Following the band introductions, Keith would amble to the microphone to sing a few numbers, then the band would play a short "in the round" set on a small center stage, and during "Sympathy for the Devil" the lights would turn bloodred. In fact, the set lists and staging cues were so strictly adhered to that for fans who attended multiple concerts the shows were reduced to the one or two variations, as in "How was Atlanta?" "Great. They played 'Sway.' "

None of this seemed to matter to Roy or Kevin, and their enthusiasm was infectious. Whenever Ronnie Wood played a hot guitar solo, or Jagger brought the crowd to its feet, Roy would turn to me and say, *"Brilliant!"* On several occasions, he handed me his binoculars. Pressing them to my face, I was able to catch little moments I was otherwise too far removed to see—a roadie crouched behind the amps tuning Richards's guitar, an exchange between Ronnie Wood and Jagger that made them laugh—as if, for those close enough to see it, a different concert was taking place.

Throughout the night, Kevin offered a highly specific running commentary, leaning over to tell me things, like "That's the first time I've seen Keith play that seventy-two Telecaster Custom in open G tuning," or "Darryl must have gone back and learned

Bill's exact bass parts on *Exile*." His observations weren't always music-related; referring to Lisa Fischer, the voluptuous black backup singer who has toured with the Stones for many years, he said, "Lisa's tits got bigger from the last tour. How'd that happen?"

During "Get Up, Stand Up," Jagger skipped across a catwalk and led everyone in the song's call-and-response chant: *"Ah-yo-O! Ah-yo-O-O!"*

When the band played "Honky Tonk Women" and Jagger sang, "I laid a divorcee in New York City," the hometown crowd screamed.

For the encore, the Stones played "You Can't Always Get What You Want," followed by "Brown Sugar." The houselights came on, confetti rained down from the rafters, and eighteen thousand people sang, *"I said yeah, yeah, yeah, woo!"* as the Stones played the outro on and on.

When the show was over, Kevin and I stood for a long moment at the railing and looked at the empty stage and the people clearing out of the arena. "Getting a last look," Kevin said, "to preserve it in my mind."

As it happened, I wasn't finished hearing Stones music that night. After the concert, I said good-bye to Kevin and walked nine blocks north to the B. B. King Blues Club, in Times Square. B. B. King's has become a popular spot to see tribute bands and aging rock acts like, say, Robin Trower or Ten Years After, whose hits have dried up but whose enthusiasm for touring has not. And on that night, as a tie-in to the Stones concert, the club had brought in a Stones tribute called Rock 'n' Roll Circus. I didn't necessarily want to hear *more* Stones music, but I did want to see Rock 'n'

Roll Circus, because the band's singer, Larry Larue, had been the original singer in Sticky Fingers before Glen took over the band.

Larry had quit the music business to become a hairdresser, but he'd recently come out of retirement after twenty years to sing Stones songs again. I'd heard lots of stories about Larry from former band members—about how he was a tireless and flamboyant performer; about how he showed up to engagements in a limousine; about how he performed wearing a pageboy wig and at the end of each show would take it off to reveal a long mane of hair, which he would whip around like a head-banger.

Gar Francis, one of the early Keiths, recalled for me the first time he met Larry, at an audition to join Sticky Fingers. Gar said, "I still remember it. I was supposed to meet Larry at another band member's house. I walked in with a guitar and sat down and Larry looked at me and—without ever hearing me play—said, 'Do you smoke cigarettes?' I said, 'Yeah.' He said, 'Do you drink bourbon?' I said, 'Yeah.' He said, 'Okay, you're in. We're playing Friday night.'"

Larry was in his forties now, but he still had the same flamboyant stage presence. That night at the B. B. King Blues Club, he was decked out in the outfit Mick Jagger wore around the time *Get Yer Ya-Ya's Out* was recorded: an American flag cape and a matching Uncle Sam top hat. When I arrived, there was hardly anyone in the club, but that didn't dampen Larry's enthusiasm. In the course of seven songs, he made three costume changes. One involved a gold sparkly blouse with matching scarf, another a leather top, and the third the American flag getup. Each time it appeared the crowd was fading, he would yell in a brassy Jersey accent, "C'mon, New York. The Stones are in the city. *Give me a hand!"* Having just seen the real Stones in Madison Square Garden, the tribute world seemed hopelessly slight.

When the show was over, I introduced myself to Larry and asked him if we could talk sometime about the early days of Sticky Fingers. One afternoon a few weeks later, we met at the Hard Rock Café in Times Square and Larry told me the story of how he became the band's first Mick. Larry was born in Jersey City and later lived in Toms River, in southern New Jersey, near the shore. In 1976, when he was twenty, he began singing in cover bands that played local fire halls and what Larry calls "shot and beer" bars—little dives that featured live music. One of the bands Larry played with, Small Change, became a big draw on account of Larry's outrageous performing style, which he described this way: "I figured if you put on enough chiffon and glitter, you were going to be a hit." Small Change used to do a set of Stones songs during their shows, and a year after the band broke up, a music manager called Larry and asked if he was still doing his Mick Jagger impersonation. The manager represented a show band called Sam the Band, whose members wore silk Quiana shirts and blended music and comedy. Sam the Band had attracted a big following in the mid-seventies, releasing an album on Casablanca Records, but by 1981 had found themselves out of style in the era of punk and new wave. At the time, the Doors tribute band Crystal Ship was selling out clubs all over the tristate area. Larry said the manager wanted to pair him with the members of Sam the Band to create a similar tribute to the Stones, who had just released *Tattoo You* and were touring that year.

Sticky Fingers happened to form during a live music boom in the Northeast—roughly a decade-long period beginning in the early seventies when bars and rock clubs were packed on most nights of the week. The good times stemmed largely from a short-lived amendment to the drinking law: during the early seventies, several states, including New Jersey and Connecticut, introduced bills lowering the legal drinking age from twenty-one to eighteen. The measure was an outgrowth of the Vietnam War, which eighteen-year-olds were being drafted to fight in, and the passage of the Twenty-sixth Amendment, which gave eighteen-year-olds the right to vote. People argued that if you could die for your country and vote for president, you should be able to drink a beer legally. As a result, a large population of young people, many of them in college or holding their first jobs, with disposable income and no responsibilities, were let loose in the bar scene. Four hundred thousand new drinkers were created in New Jersey alone. The change in the law was a windfall for bar owners and rock and roll musicians, especially in New Jersey, where the mix of blue-collar factory towns, numerous colleges, and the shore assured there would be plenty of young people looking to go out and have a good time and listen to live music. Bars and clubs flourished: Mother's in Wayne, the Lighthouse Rock Disco in Hopatcong, the Starland Ballroom in Sayreville, Colonel's Garter in Neptune, the Fountain Casino on Route 35, the Soap Factory on Route 46, Zaffy's in Piscataway, the Final Exam in Randolph, the Best Inn in Linden, the Beach House in Point Pleasant, the Fast Lane and the Stone Pony in Asbury Park, the Chatterbox in Seaside Heights, Dunes 'Till Dawn in Margate—and every one featured live music. Each week, the *Aquarian,* New Jersey's rock paper, printed concert listings, page after page of them.

It was a great time to be a young, good-looking, longhaired

guy in a rock band. You could make a living as a musician just by playing in a popular cover act. Sticky Fingers performed four or five nights a week, packing all the big clubs, like Hammerheads on Long Island and the Agora Ballroom in West Hartford, Connecticut. Larry quit his job as a salesclerk in a department store and became a full-time rock and roll singer. "I remember one evening an agent handed me more money than most people make in a month," Larry said. "There was so much money floating around. Even a guy pumping gas or working retail could buy a few grams of coke to party with on the weekends." Other tribute bands began to sprout up, like Nursery Cryme, a tribute to Genesis, and Montreux, a tribute to Deep Purple *and* Rainbow. This was also the period when the Blushing Brides were selling out clubs around New England. A man I spoke to named Bruce Freedman, who handled the bookings for the Agora Ballroom in Hartford during this period, told me, "I'll give you an example of how big these tribute bands were. Crystal Ship came in and we put them in the big room at the Agora, which held four thousand people. This was in 1980. I ended up giving them seventy-five percent of the door. They walked out of there with ten thousand dollars in cash. And these guys had no record out. They were never going to have a record. They were a clone band!"

When Larry joined Sticky Fingers, the band's manager told him the group would eventually perform not just in New Jersey but all over the country. Larry believed he would become a rock star, although he didn't write his own songs and had no real plan for how stardom would happen. After a year or two of playing the same New York–New Jersey clubs, he realized the band's manager didn't have the connections to take Sticky Fingers national, and the excessive number of local shows began to temper the band's appeal. By then, the live-music scene was beginning to change around him. In the early eighties, a number of politicians, along with groups like Mothers Against Drunk Driving, lobbied to restore the legal drinking age to twenty-one, arguing that drunk-driving accidents and deaths had spiked. On January 1, 1983, New Jersey's legal drinking age was reinstated to twenty-one; that same year, Connecticut raised its legal age to twenty. Some states held out, but the federal government pledged to reduce what one official called "carnage on the highways." In 1984, President Reagan signed into law a bill that denied federal highway funds to any state whose drinking age remained under twenty-one. Soon, all fifty states complied. Other changes were taking place, too. Club owners began more and more to replace live bands with DJs as a more cost-effective way to entertain people. And the popularity of hip-hop would soon create a generation whose idea of going out on a Saturday night centered around dancing at a club, not seeing a rock band. "It used to be, 'Let's go see Rat Race Choir out on Long Island—I know the bouncer,' " Kevin Gleeson once lamented. "Now it's DJs and house music." Kevin and Glen, Maurice and Shane, Larry Larue—all the musicians I met had vivid memories of seeing live music alongside hundreds of other rock fans in a packed club. When they performed now to a half-empty room, their faces seemed to convey a sense of bewilderment—as if they had stepped away from a riotous party for a minute and returned only to find everyone had gone home.

At his manager's suggestion, Larry began doing half Stones, half David Bowie to enliven the act, and the crowds returned briefly. But Sticky Fingers had run its course. Larry formed a Top 40 metal cover band called Cocktail Choir, then drifted out of music altogether, where he remained for nearly two decades, until he sang at a benefit show organized on behalf of one of the original members of Sticky Fingers, who'd been diagnosed with cancer. A lot of old Sticky Fingers fans attended the benefit and the experience made Larry realize how much he missed performing. The night at the B. B. King Blues Club was only his fifth show since reemerging on the tribute scene.

Larry was aware of Glen's version of Sticky Fingers, and I asked him if it was strange to know the band has continued in his absence, trading on the reputation he'd helped to forge. "The problem is that a lot of people I've met go to see Sticky Fingers thinking they're going to see me," he said, then added, "I actually met Glen once on Bleecker Street. After Sticky Fingers broke up, one of my guitar players, Gar Francis, joined Glen's Sticky Fingers. So Gar invited me down to the Rock 'n' Roll Café one night to see them play. I went to the dressing room and Glen just completely ignored me. Just turned around and walked out. I thought, What is this, battling Micks? After a while, it's so pretentious." Larry laughed. "Okay, you look like Mick Jagger and I look like Mick Jagger, too. Are we going to drop our pants and get a ruler out? Is that how we're going to decide who's the better Mick?"

9

On occasions when I wasn't driving around the country with the members of Sticky Fingers or the Blushing Brides, or paying large sums of money to see the Stones in concert, I often went to see other tribute bands. I drove to Delaware one night to see the Led Zeppelin tribute Zoso. At a bar in Manhattan I saw the Aerosmith band Draw the Line, whose singer, Neill Byrnes, so strikingly resembles Steven Tyler that he has wondered if he is Tyler's illegitimate son. And one Saturday morning, I returned to the B. B. King Blues Club in Times Square—this time for "Beatles Brunch," a weekly event that includes an all-you-can-eat buffet, lots of tourists, and music by the Beatles tribute Strawberry Fields.

One of the tribute bands I was most interested in seeing was Dark Star Orchestra, the group that re-creates exact Grateful Dead shows—say, Red Rocks Amphitheater, August 30, 1978. It was an approach made possible by the archival rigor peculiar to Deadheads, who bootlegged hundreds of Dead concerts and scrupulously compiled four decades' worth of set lists. In retracing the Dead's long, strange trip, Dark Star Orchestra has built a loyal following among the kinds of people who enjoy smoking pot and listening to twenty-minute tribal drum jams. By the time I saw the band, in 2005, they were playing 150 concerts a year, a lot of them in concert halls and soft-seat theaters, and traveling across the country in a coach bus. On tour, the seven band members are accompanied by a road crew that includes two sound engineers, a lighting technician, a tour manager, a bus driver, and a merchandise guy who sells Dark Star Orchestra shirts, hats, posters, sew-on patches, compact discs, and DVDs. The band's gross earnings exceed one million dollars a year. Dark Star Orchestra also employs a publicist, which I discovered when I tried to arrange a meeting with the band before one of its concerts in Englewood, New Jersey. I was surprised to be negotiating with a publicist for access to a tribute band, but I was more astonished to learn an interview might not be possible; the group was nearing the end of an East Coast tour, I was told, and the musicians tended to get grumpy after six weeks on the road. "You know how artists are," the publicist said apologetically. "I'll see what I can do."

When, an hour or so before show time, I arrived at the venue, a handsome performing arts center in downtown Englewood, the lobby was empty except for a young guy with a ponytail unpacking T-shirts from a crate. The band's publicist had arranged for me to be met by the road manager, a woolly-bearded man named Tiny, who carried a clipboard and handed me a backstage pass with the band's initials, "DSO," printed on the front in a purple psychedelic-looking font and the word *Press* handwritten underneath in ink. Tiny said that the band was unavailable for interviews at the moment but that I could talk with their sound engineer. Speaking into a walkie-talkie clipped to his shoulder, he produced a friendly, professorial-looking guy named Cameron Blietz.

Aside from doing the band's sound, Cameron chronicled the group's adventures in a travelogue, "Road Rash," which he posts on Dark Star Orchestra's Web site, and he seemed to view life through painted white lines. "We're on the road a good chunk of the time we're on this rock," he said with a philosophical tone as we sat in the back of the empty theater, behind the myriad dials and knobs of the soundboard.

I asked him about the band's coach bus, which was parked outside, looking like a stray from a Greyhound fleet.

Cameron said the band had been leasing the coach but had recently bought it outright, fitting the interior with twelve sleeping bunks. "Basically, my bunk is my apartment for two hundred days a year," he said. "If I put my arms out like this"—he spread his arms—"that's the edge of my bunk, and if I put my elbows at my sides, my fingertips touch the ceiling. I'm like canned goods." He chuckled. "The funny thing is that now I sleep better on the bus. I just have to figure out how to get my bed at home to go sixty-five miles an hour and occasionally hit a rumble strip, and I'll sleep great."

We talked a while longer, during which time Cameron explained how Dark Star Orchestra had formed in 1997, when members from various jam bands and Dead cover groups in Chicago came together to play weekly at a club called Martyrs'. The band went from being a popular draw at Martyrs' to doing brief tours of jam band–friendly places like Colorado, and then to touring the country year-round. Cameron said that a few months earlier, the group's founding keyboardist had died of a heart attack on tour, which saddened the band members but also freaked them out, because the Grateful Dead's keyboard players notoriously had a history of dying, too. When I walked back out to the lobby, Dark Star Orchestra fans were beginning to stream in. They were dressed for the most part in tie-dyed shirts, or T-shirts printed with a picture of Jerry Garcia's face, or of Bob Marley, and they wore baggy jeans and corduroy pants and hemp necklaces and floppy wool caps with cable-knit stitching and Birkenstock sandals, and they smelled of patchouli and marijuana. Some looked too young to have seen the Grateful Dead in concert, and many more looked like aging Deadheads happy to be back in circulation. When the Grateful Dead disbanded after Jerry Garcia's death, in 1995, the traveling carnival that had built up around them for decades vanished. The remaining members formed other groups and continued to tour, but they had played Grateful Dead songs for thirty years and naturally wanted to try something different, and anyway, it wasn't the same without Garcia. Then Dark Star Orchestra came along, replicating exact Dead concerts, and revived the whole hibernating Deadhead culture.

In the lobby, the band's merchandise was arranged for sale on a card table: Dark Star Orchestra ball caps (twenty dollars, available in black or cream), a sweatshirt with dates from the current tour printed on the back (thirty-five dollars), a *Live at the Fillmore* DVD; a three-CD set commemorating the band's one thousandth show. Nick, the merch guy, had straight black hair and Native American–looking features and was dressed in worn jeans and a blue button-up shirt that said SPRINGFIELD PD, CHIEF OF POLICE

CLANCY WIGGUM. Had it been fifteen years earlier, he would probably have been following the Grateful Dead in a VW bus, selling hemp necklaces in stadium parking lots to pay his way to the next show. But in the Dead's absence, he'd spent the past two years on the road with Dark Star Orchestra. "I'm twenty-two, man," he said, grinning. "I'm living it up."

Nick regaled me with some of his road adventures; they were mostly the sort of rambling, you-had-to-be-there tales stoners tell. In San Francisco, he'd hung out with the counterculture artist Stanley Mouse, and on tour in Pennsylvania he and the band had had a night off, so they drove to Philadelphia to see the Australian Pink Floyd Show. The idea of a Grateful Dead tribute band taking a break from their tour to see a Pink Floyd tribute band made me think again about how the tribute world is a parallel rock and roll universe. "They're awesome," Nick said of the Pink Floyd band. "They even have the inflatable pig from *Animals*. Do yourself a favor—go see those guys."

A heavyset guy with a baby face walked into the lobby. Nick appeared to recognize him and said, "See, I love it. We know people all over. *Yeaaaah!* Hey Prescott, what's up, man?"

"Hey, dude," Prescott said, walking over to the table. "So, can I get a bootleg copy of tonight's concert?"

"The first batch will be ready five minutes after the show," Nick said. "It's twenty dollars and you get three CDs. Just sign up, dude."

A tall, floppy-haired, preppy-looking guy accompanied by a woman stopped by to say hello. He said he'd driven from Connecticut to see Dark Star Orchestra. "I follow these guys all over, man," he said to me. "I can go out to San Fran. Get a hotel. See these guys play the Great American Music Hall. Party well." I asked him how long he'd been listening to the Grateful Dead. "I first saw the Dead in '82. I was just a kid. I had no money, but damn I had a good time. Now I got a little extra bucks. I can get a nice room, have a nice dinner with the girl." Walking into the theater, he held up his tickets and grinned. "Front-row seats, by the way."

On the night I saw Dark Star Orchestra, it was the band's 1,165th show. I know this because the band members maintain a meticulous count. They also keep records relating to the specific Dead concerts they've reenacted, and when and where. That way, they can ensure that they don't play the same Dead show, or a show from the same era, or one with a similar set of songs, more than once in the same city. It has become a bit of a game between the band and its fans to figure out what show Dark Star Orchestra is re-creating on a given night. There are all sorts of visual clues, which seasoned Deadheads can spot. For instance, if only one drummer is onstage the show dates to between 1971 and 1974, when Mickey Hart briefly left the band. (It could also be before late 1967, before Hart joined, but Dark Star Orchestra doesn't do sixties shows, because the band hasn't found someone up to the task of playing "Pigpen" McKernan and also because the Dead did a lot of acid in that period and it's difficult to re-create those performances.) An expert Deadhead can further home in on the date by paying careful attention to the set list and the song arrangements and running times and even the instruments onstage—by knowing that, say, the keyboardist Brent Mydland used a Hammond B-3, but earlier Dead keyboard players did not, so if a B-3 is onstage, the show must date to after spring of 1979, when Mydland joined the band.

As it happened, the Dead show Dark Star Orchestra performed in Englewood was Mershon Auditorium, Ohio State University, September 30, 1976—a two-drummer night that also featured a Donna Jean Godchaux vocal. In the early part of the concert, Dark Star's Donna Jean, a sleepy-eyed brunette, split her time between harmonizing and dancing the twirly way hippie girls do. The musicians hadn't gone out of their way to look like the members of the Grateful Dead, but they seemed to resemble them anyway, as if by transference. The Jerry guy had frizzy hair worn in a ponytail and a beatific air about him, while the Bob guy had Bob Weir's rugged good looks and nasal vocal register. The keyboard player—who, if my time line of Dead keyboardists serves me right, would have been playing the role of Keith God- chaux—sported a red bandanna and was dressed head to toe in denim, like the guys from those old '70s Preservation Society TV commercials. Musically, the likeness was even more extraordinary: Dark Star Orchestra had the same bright, crisp, heavily EQ'd sound the Dead did in concert, the same melded vocal harmonies, the same slightly seasick rhythmic meter, like a boat that feels as if it's about to tip over but never does.

I watched from a seat midway to the stage. In the same row was a middle-aged man who had brought his young son. It was clear by the way the man was intently studying the musicians on- stage that the Grateful Dead's music meant a great deal to him and that he wanted to share it with his boy. But the boy was fixated on a handheld video game in his lap.

When the band finished the first set, I walked out to the lobby and stood around for a few minutes, then went backstage. The musicians and a few audience members and friends were standing around in a storage area piled with theatrical rigging.

The keyboard player wearing the bandanna was talking animatedly to a blond woman about a guy he knew who used to sell LSD and I overheard him say, "So the cops were gonna bust him and to avoid getting arrested he ate a sheet. Two hundred and fifty hits! To this day—and this was many, many years ago—he's *completely out of his mind.*" I struck up a conversation with one of the drummers, a low-key guy named Dino English. Dino said that before joining Dark Star Orchestra, he'd drummed in another Dead tribute, The Schwag, in St. Louis, where he lives. Dino said the members of Dark Star Orchestra live all over and come together for tours. "The guy who does Jerry doesn't even have a home," he said. "He has a camper, and when our tours end, he just travels around until it's time to go on the road again."

I asked him if his relationship to the Grateful Dead's music had changed since he'd joined Dark Star Orchestra.

"It's hard to separate yourself from the scholarship sometimes and just listen to the music for enjoyment," Dino said.

In fact, Dark Star Orchestra seemed to represent a sort of apotheosis of the tribute concept in terms of how faithfully they copied another group's music. In order to re-create the Grateful Dead's live performing career, the musicians had to commit to memory hundreds of concerts spanning three decades, and limn the subtle differences between each of them. I later had a phone conversation with the band's Jerry, John Kadlecik, who explained in considerable detail how the Dead might have played a song in a number of ways over their long career. "A good example is 'Loose Lucy,'" he said. "When it first appeared in the live repertoire, probably about a year before it came out on the *Mars Hotel* album, it had that slow, chunky R&B beat. When they recorded it, they changed it into a more up-tempo beat, with a little bit of swing to it. That's the way they played it for the rest of seventy-four. But then they dropped it completely when Mickey came back, and it didn't show up again until the late eighties. And when it showed up in the late eighties, they had taken it back to its original form, slow, with a little swing to it." He went on: "Another good example is 'Dire Wolf.' On the album, it's in the key of A. In the early seventies, the Dead really opened up this one particular beat, and they were using it in a lot of songs: 'Ramble on Rose,' 'He's Gone,' 'Dire Wolf.' It was a slow beat, but with a little bit of swing to it. It had these busy inside figures so the dancers could groove, even though the actual beat seemed like it should be a slow song. Then in the late seventies, they changed the key to C on 'Dire Wolf' and changed the form. You still had the A verse, the B verse, and the two C verses, but then they solo over the A verse, repeating one or two or three times, and then go into the last verse over the A form. No more extra solo."

In addition to learning all the songs the Dead performed live, and the way those songs changed with repeated playing, the members of Dark Star Orchestra also had to learn how to *improvise* in the style of the Dead in order to play free-form instrumental jams like "Drums" and "Space." Dino said the musicians sometimes spend hours on the tour bus deconstructing Dead shows: they cross-reference set lists, analyze photos of the Dead in concert, study Grateful Dead reference books like *The Taper's Compendium* series, which documents every known Dead bootleg. The band also maintains an extensive collection of bootleg tapes stored in a basement in Illinois—a sort of Deadhead Library of Alexandria. "We view ourselves as an orchestra," Dino said. "I mean, these songs are really concertos, you know." I'd heard this argument before, from Steve Leber, the creator of *Beatlemania*. He said tribute bands were no different from classical orchestras. Both perform the music of great composers; it just so happens that in the case of tribute bands, the composers are named Lennon and Jagger and Garcia, not Mozart or Handel, and they haven't been dead two hundred years to be properly canonized. The argument seemed at once convincing and also off base, because so much of rock and roll relies on elements beyond the musical notes, like style and attitude. When an orchestra performs a Mozart concerto, they don't dress up in powdered wigs and velvet knickers.

A low-hanging cloud of pot smoke had blanketed the theater by the start of the band's second set. The aisles filled with twirling hippie dancers; a teenage boy consumed too much of some substance and passed out in front of the stage, briefly stopping the concert. As the band started in on the chunky rhythm of "Scarlet Begonias," I felt the room grow stuffy and claustrophobic. Watching the musicians, I began to think about Dark Star Orchestra's ambition to re-create the Grateful Dead's live performing career, and the immensity of the task and the obsessive attention to detail required. The Grateful Dead performed live more than any other rock band in history, an estimated 2,500 concerts over a thirty-year period. And because the musicians were given so heavily to improvisation, they never played a song in the same way twice, creating a near-infinite number of notes and chords and rhythms. In listening to the thousand or more bootleg concert recordings, in deconstructing every guitar lick, keyboard trill, and cymbal splash and then placing them in the context of the whole again, in arriving at a complete mastery of the band's music, given the variables of age and lineup changes and whatever chemicals the musicians ingested on a given night, you could lose yourself. You could disappear.

That evening with Dark Star Orchestra reminded me of something Kevin Gleeson said one day while we were driving to a Sticky Fingers show. Discussing the hazards of impersonating someone as self-destructive as Keith Richards, he said he was careful not to develop "tributitus." If it were listed in a psychology reference book, which it isn't, tributitus might be defined as "a mental disorder known to affect some tribute musicians, in which the performer begins to identify too closely with the famous rock star he or she is portraying." As in most disorders, there are varying degrees of severity: in a mild case of tributitus, tribute performers may display an inflated ego and demand unmerited rock star–like treatment ("I said a stretch limo!"). Offstage, they begin to exhibit the surface character traits of their onstage character. Russ Forster once told me about a few cases of tributitus he'd come across in the course of filming his documentary about tribute bands, including what he called "a really unfortunate" encounter with the singer of a Doors tribute band. "I'd heard they were a great band, so I called the singer on the phone and made my pitch to shoot some footage," Forster said. "The response I got was unbelievable. He said he was willing to be involved *only* if he could see all the footage I shot, and *only* if he had final cut on the movie. Then he said he wasn't sure he wanted to be associated with the tribute scene anyway because he was working on a solo record that was going to be the solo record Jim Morrison would have made had he not died. He said it was going to blow everyone out of the water." Forster also had two oddly similar encounters with Eddie Van Halens, each of whom insisted he draft a legal contract before filming. "At the time, it freaked me out to have two different Eddie Van Halens from two different bands do the same thing," Forster said. "People have since told me the actual Eddie Van Halen is somewhat that way." (There is, of course, a chicken-and-egg element here: does someone gravitate to the role of Eddie Van Halen because he shares similar personality traits or did portraying Eddie Van Halen give rise to those qualities?)

In advanced cases of tributitus, real life and the tribute world become hopelessly blurred and the performer loses himself entirely in the role. One such case of late-stage tributitus is evident in another documentary about tribute bands, *Tribute,* which profiles, among others, a KISS band from California called Larger than Life. In the film, the band's leader, a quietly intense man named Andy, earns his band mates' admiration for the way he "becomes" Gene Simmons. Scenes of Andy wiggling his overlarge tongue and breathing fire in a parking lot illustrate the point. The narrative shifts to other tribute bands and, later, when the film returns to Larger than Life, the other members appear shellshocked. In the interim, Andy apparently set fire to his house, jumped through a window, and was carted off in an ambulance; he later renounces KISS as devil music. "I think he got sucked up by his ego," one of Andy's band mates theorizes. "Everybody telling him he looked like Gene Simmons and everything—he really started to believe it. But then he has to come back down to reality when he goes home. He may be Gene Simmons in his mind, but his old lady's going, 'Take out the fucking garbage.' "

There are other, less dramatic complications to being in a

tribute band—principally, suppressing your own personality in order to mimic someone else. Marty Paglione, the original drummer in Larry Larue's version of Sticky Fingers, once told me, "A tribute band is the most narrow road you could ever be on. If the public really loves it, it's because they love the original. You're just making them think you're the original. You're a surrogate to the real thing and you get a weird, sickening feeling doing it." Some tribute performers try to retain a part of themselves in their role, like Larry Larue theatrically revealing his hair as a declaration of self. But many musicians feel the point of being in a rock band is to express your creativity, and they are unable to reconcile the idea of deliberately copying another person's music. When I saw Zoso in Delaware, the band was playing with a new drummer because the longtime drummer had recently quit to pursue his own music. "He could never get over the idea that people weren't knowing him for him," the band's singer, Matt Jernigan, told me. Jernigan has a more generous view of tribute bands, shaped by the frustrating years he spent in various on-the-cusp original bands. He said he tried to persuade the drummer to reconsider. "I told him, it's about being able to play music and make a living and keep fulfilling the passion you've had since you were a child," Jernigan said. "Another thing I kept telling him is that we're not like athletes, where, if you're a running back in high school and you score twenty touchdowns, you're going to college, and if you do it there, you're going to the pros. Music is a far less merited business. You could be the greatest musician in the world and be playing in your basement forever. The point is to be out there onstage, because you never know who's in the audience. I never thought I'd be singing in a Led Zeppelin tribute band, but at least I'm not doing something I would hate. I'm playing music."

The first musicians to navigate the strange currents of tribute band life were the original cast members of *Beatlemania,* who were also the first to experience the odd fame that comes with it, predicated as it is on someone else's fame and accomplishments. Joe Pecorino recalled to me the internal dilemma that followed each autograph request: should he sign his own name or John Lennon's? People know that tribute musicians are mimics, of course, but they often seem to willfully forget. They routinely address band members by their character's name, calling out "Keith" or "Mick," and women sometimes sleep with a tribute performer because they are attracted to the rock star he portrays. One day, at the height of *Beatlemania's* popularity, Joe Pecorino and Mitch Weissman were chased through midtown Manhattan by a pack of screaming girls, as if living a scene from *A Hard Day's Night.* At a tribute show, a mass suspension of reality takes place between performer and audience; for a brief period, the tribute band becomes real. That sort of reality blur could create an identity crisis in even the most mentally centered people.

During *Beatlemania's* theatrical run, an odd transference occurred as the cast members began to play out their stage roles in real life. Mitch Weissman, like Paul McCartney, was looked upon as the band leader but was superficially eager to assuage any tensions, while Joe Pecorino possessed John Lennon's rebellious streak. On the surface, the two men were friends, but a subtle rivalry existed between them, as one did in the Lennon-McCartney partnership. Justin McNeill, like Ringo, was an afterthought, while Les Fradkin, as if reliving George Harrison's life in simulation, felt overshadowed by his band mates and minimized creatively, and argued for a greater role in the show, which was impossible; the script had already been written, by the Beatles themselves. Around the time that *Beatlemania* opened in Los Angeles, Steve Leber grew concerned that the cast members were taking drugs and in-fighting and sent Kenny Laguna, the original musical director, to spy on them. "I would see the head trips and the craziness," Kenny Laguna said. "I wasn't a sage or anything, but I told Leber, 'I think you're doing damage to these kids.' Steve would say, 'They're driving around in a Mercedes. It's a great opportunity.' I said, 'No. I think their brains are getting sucked out of their heads.' It's hard enough to be a legitimate rock star and not get all mixed up. These guys had all that going on, but on top of it, they weren't themselves. They were characters."

Beatlemania remains, decades later, a vivid and fateful experience for the musicians involved. When the show ended its run on Broadway in 1979, a few cast members went on to successful careers in the music industry, like Marshall Crenshaw, who was a John Lennon. But many remain tethered to *Beatlemania* well into middle age. They reunite periodically in the manner of championship sports teams and perform in the dozens of Beatles tribute bands that have sprouted, like a cottage industry, in the years since the show ended. According to an Internet fan site dedicated to *Beatlemania,* Tom Teeley, the George of Bunk Three, "still finds time to perform today with Classical Mystery Tour"; Alan LeBoeuf of Bunk Three "remains a very busy Paul." The John of Bunk Three, Mark Vaccacio, is now the George in Strawberry Fields, the band that performs at the B. B. King Blues Club. Randy Clark and Bobby Taylor (John and Ringo in Bunk Two respectively) have both performed in the tribute Rain, entertaining cruise ship audiences, as have Joey Curatolo (Paul) and Ralph Castelli (another Ringo) of Bunk Four—all of them squeezing their aging bodies into black Chesterfield suits like the ones the

Beatles wore as twenty-two-year-olds. In fact, there were so many former cast members trading off the *Beatlemania* name that in the early nineties it gave rise to what has since come to be called the "Beatle Wars," as bands undercut one another for gigs and musicians claimed false associations to the Broadway show to increase their chances of being booked.

As for the original cast, Joe Pecorino rarely performs as John Lennon anymore and Justin McNeill is said to have left the Beatles world altogether. But Les Fradkin still tours with his group, the Boys from Beatlemania. Taking advantage of the Beatles' long-standing lawsuit with Steve Jobs over rights to the name Apple, he also records and sells George Harrison songs on Apple iTunes. "I will absolutely have the Internet market cornered on George Harrison songs by the end of the year," he told me. (Fradkin also writes, self-produces, and self-releases his own albums, and he sent me several of them, including *Reality—The Rock Opera,* a rock opera about reality TV.) The star of *Beatlemania,* Mitch Weissman, lives in Los Angeles now and works at Sam Ash Music. In the years after the show, he cowrote a few songs with Gene Simmons and played in his own bands. But he always drifted back to the *Beatlemania* orbit, where for many he remains a star. I met Weissman for breakfast one morning in Hollywood and was surprised to see that although he's gained some weight, he still looks remarkably like Paul McCartney—better than the real version, in fact. He had just returned from playing a Beatles gig in upstate New York with a band called Cast of Beatlemania. "I told my friend Carlo, who leads the band, this is like our version of the male hunting trip," he said jovially. "We go out and kill the audience."

A tribute band featuring all four original cast members

would no doubt be a big draw on the casino and cruise ship circuit, and there has been some talk about reuniting. But for many reasons, some scheduling, some interpersonal, the original cast of *Beatlemania* has never reunited onstage—just like the Beatles.

10

One weekend in early October, after the Stones tour had passed through New England and made its way across the South—to cities like Charlottesville, Virginia (where a concert was briefly stopped because of a bomb threat), and Durham, North Carolina—the Blushing Brides returned from their two-month hiatus. The band was booked to play two shows in Massachusetts, the first being a fiftieth birthday party for somebody's uncle Leo, at a place called Kathleen's Function Facility in Walpole. It was around this time that I realized the Brides were in the midst of a run of bad shows.

There had been the "Fake Fest" in Atlantic City and the engagement at the club in Cape Cod that went bankrupt, and the gig at White's, where the band performed down the hall from a high school reunion. I imagine that when Maurice formed the Brides in 1978 with Paul Martin, he didn't plan on singing Stones covers at a birthday party for a guy named Uncle Leo twenty-seven years later. He expected to *replace* Mick Jagger as the singer of the *next* Rolling Stones. Of the tribute performers I'd met, Maurice was the one who most clearly possessed the gifts necessary to have done so. He was an exceptional front man—an old-school, give-it-all-you've-got, R&B showman, a rock and roll defibrillator, able to breathe life into dead crowds. There were times when I watched him onstage and felt that he sang Stones songs better than Jagger himself. The fact that he wasn't playing to crowded stadiums, or singing his own hit songs, or even playing a tribute fest in Rotterdam, must have caused him a certain amount of resentment and no doubt contributed to his visible frustration. It was a frustration, I felt, born of unfulfilled promise.

I was contemplating all of this during the four-hour drive to Massachusetts with the band that Friday morning in October. By now, I was intimately familiar with this trip to New England: the heavy traffic clog of I-95 as it cuts through Stamford and New Haven; the disorienting sensation of seeing the same McDonald's-dominated rest stop every fifteen miles; the desolate stretches of eastern Connecticut and southern Rhode Island; the sudden rush up to Providence, then into Massachusetts. I-95 North seemed to be a sort of trade route for Stones tribute bands.

The ride passed with its usual sights and sounds. At one point, Maurice motioned to a station wagon passing alongside us and said, "That looks nice. I need to get a station wagon for the dog."

"For the dog?" Shane said in a dubious tone.

"Yeah," Maurice said. "Right now, I have a Ford Focus and it's too damn small. The dog is ninety pounds."

"I'm a hundred and eighty pounds," Shane said, "and I'm sitting in the front seat just fine."

"My dog licks its vagina," Maurice said. "Do *you* lick your vagina?"

Shane smirked and said, "I'd lick my vagina if I had one."

The conversation shifted to the Stones tour. It turned out that Kerry Muldoon had attended the two concerts I had: opening night at Fenway Park and the show at Madison Square Garden. "After Fenway, everyone was going, 'Oh my God, the B stage was so cool,' " Kerry said from the backseat of the van, referring to the point during each concert when the Stones performed on the movable stage. "They've been doing that B stage for the last three tours. I feel like I've been watching the same show."

"You know what?" Shane said. "They need somebody like Kramer there. Like last night, I'm watching *Seinfeld* and the girl's nose is fucked up and everyone is going, 'It looks great,' and Kramer says, 'You got butchered.' The Stones need Kramer there going, 'That part stinks.' "

"What they need," Maurice said, "is a soloist, someone like Mick Taylor instead of Ronnie Wood with his slide-guitar bullshit. Ronnie is looking bad, too, man. If that guy weighs eighty pounds . . ."

"Incidentally," Kerry said, "at the Fenway show, it was hot and I didn't feel well, so during the encore I said to my friend Jill, 'Let's go stand in the back.' I leave my seat. There's an empty corridor. One person is standing in the corridor. Who do you think it was?" Kerry winced melodramatically. "*Glen Carroll!* And he was dressed in a Mick Jagger outfit. The studded pants. The Capezio shoes. *I swear to God!* Thirty-seven thousand people at the concert, I hadda see him. My night hadda be ruined."

Around Providence, the drive began to drag. To lighten the mood, Shane said, "The guy that I played with in the Alice Cooper band, Nick, well, he was a big pot smoker. So whenever we went on a road trip, he used to measure distances in joints. Like, you'd say, 'Hey, Nick, how long a ride is it to this gig?' and he'd go, 'Ahh, it's about a two-joint ride.' If it was a short trip, it might only be a one-joint ride." Shane chuckled. "I used to love that." He paused. "This drive is like a three-joint ride."

The band reached Walpole in the late afternoon. Kerry Muldoon had made reservations at a Holiday Inn Express. When Maurice pulled into the hotel parking lot, everyone piled out of the van and found their rooms. A few hours later, the band was back in the van, headed to Kathleen's Function Facility. On the way Maurice put a CD into the van's stereo and cued up "Rough Justice," the first single from the new Stones album. The Stones had been playing the song, an up-tempo rocker with a mean slide guitar lick, on tour, and Maurice wanted the Brides to learn it so the band could incorporate new material into its shows.

As the van drove through a neighborhood of old houses with showcase lawns, everyone listened in silence, trying to pick up the changes.

"It's rough justice on ya," Mick Jagger sang.

Maurice leaned into the speaker. "What key is it in?"

"E," Shane said.

"Okay," Maurice said. "Then it's an A harp. It'll sound good with a nasty, dirty harp over top."

"It's rough justice on ya."

"Repeats there," Maurice said.

"You're going to have to trust me . . ."

"No bridge," Maurice said, and Shane nodded.

Another song from the new Stones record came on—this one a beautiful acoustic ballad called "Streets of Love." During the chorus, the music swelled and Jagger sang in a falsetto. Maurice fell in, too, trying to wrap his voice around the high notes.

"And I-I-I-I-I-I I walk the streets of love and they're full of tears," the two sang, Maurice and Mick Jagger harmonizing together.

Kathleen's Function Facility was in the basement of a squat brick bar just off downtown. Maurice pulled into the parking lot. When he saw the building's worn facade, he said, wearily, "How many shitholes like this have I pulled up to?"

Inside, the room was long, low-ceilinged, warmly lit, with a small bar in the back and sound monitors arranged in a corner to suggest a space for the musicians (there was no stage). Uncle Leo's family and friends sat at tables with white tablecloths, finishing off plates of catered pasta, and the room had the starchy smell of an Italian grandmother's kitchen.

One of Leo's nephews stood up and good-naturedly roasted his uncle about turning fifty, then announced the Brides. (The band had stopped by the club earlier to set up their equipment and do a sound check.) A group of small children sat Indian-style on the floor in front of the band, wide-eyed.

Maurice, dressed in black jeans and a tight black T-shirt that showed off his muscled physique, stepped to the microphone.

"Hello. We want to thank you for bringing us," he said, in a tone of slightly forced cheer. "You seem like a very nice, happy family." Pause. "I watched the Red Sox game"—the Red Sox had lost to the Chicago White Sox that day and were eliminated from the play-offs—"and I know you're bummed out. We'll try to cheer you up."

Maurice counted off and the band launched into "Brown Sugar," a good number to dance to. But the audience, weighted with a big meal, was satisfied to sit and watch.

Over the course of the evening, Maurice made a valiant effort to put on a lively show, playfully joking with the kids at the foot of the stage, leading the audience in singing "Happy Birthday" to Uncle Leo, dashing into the crowd to pull two women onto the dance floor. As the night went on, though, he grew sullen and withdrawn. He scolded Daniel Hoffenberg for not starting a song quickly enough. And, in the style of a high school football coach dogging an overweight lineman for lack of hustle, he got in Rodney Ledbetter's face for not hitting the cymbals more forcefully. Rodney glared back at Maurice evilly. In the second set, Maurice mostly kept his back to the crowd and said little, finishing the engagement with a workmanlike efficiency. When the show was over, he stormed into the band's dressing room, slumped against a wall, and held his head in his hands miserably.

"You know, it wasn't just the band last night," Shane said the next day, after the Brides checked out of the Holiday Inn Express, breakfasted at a Bickfords, then drove fifty miles south and checked into the Swansea Motor Inn on Route 6 in Swansea. The band was performing that night in nearby Fall River. That afternoon, Shane and Lee Boice borrowed the van to drive to

Wal-Mart and buy batteries for their guitar pedals; on the way, they discussed the reasons for Maurice's bad mood.

It was raining steadily, and Shane drove hunched over the wheel, concentrating on the slick highway. Everyone was already resigned to the fact that the show that night was another lost cause, because people tended to stay home during bad weather.

"It was looking out at that wedding-type scene," Shane said, "with the little kids and the moms and dads and grandmas."

Lee Boice groaned. "It's just a douche situation," he said. "You always tell yourself, I'll never play in a wedding band. It's like, wow, if my cool friends could see me now."

"I knew it would fucking break him down," Shane said. "He was so disgusted. Usually on nights he doesn't want to play, he'll talk for five minutes between songs. He couldn't even bring himself to keep that going."

The rain picked up and Shane clicked the wipers to high. "If I was Daniel, I'd have quit already," Shane said. "Soon as he did the first gig where Moe went"—and here Shane's voice became a drill sergeant–like bark—" *'C'mon. Start the next song. Now! Now! Now!'* I would've said, 'Listen, if you want songs to start bang-bang-bang, give me a set list and I'll tape it to my amp and I'll know what guitar I need and I'll start the song.' " (Daniel, in fact, was a fine blues player, but having replaced Paul Martin he was a substitute for another guy, fated to disappoint Maurice.)

"Yeah, man," Lee said. "Why does he do that to the guy? It's like, 'Don't tune. Just play!' What are you, crazy?"

Shane shook his head as if to say, What can you do? "Singers," he said.

————

When the band drove to Fall River that night, their fears about a bad turnout were borne out: the town had the foggy, eerily isolated feel of a *Twilight Zone* location. Not a soul on the streets.

Maurice parked the van in an alley alongside the venue, a restaurant and bar that was formerly the Eagle but was now under new management and called the New Eagle. The musicians unloaded their equipment in a drizzle and shuffled up the steps; in the stairwell was a promotional poster with a color photo of Maurice, sweaty and shirtless, next to the words "The Blushing Brides, Voyeurism Tour 2005."

The New Eagle was surprisingly grand inside, with the sort of high domed ceiling and ornate balcony boxes of an old vaudeville theater, or one of the hippie ballrooms of the sixties. The place was faded, but it could still be made magical again with a great band and a packed house. At nine o'clock, nearing show time, there were maybe twenty-five people in the whole place.

One of the things that most interested me about the Blushing Brides was their singular career path—the way they had started as a tribute band, then graduated into a band whose members wrote and recorded their own songs, then regressed *back* to being a tribute band. Having set out to become the next Stones, and having worked tirelessly toward that end, the Brides had abandoned the notion when it was at last in the realm of possibility. Now, years later, Maurice was performing for small crowds in places like the New Eagle, where his considerable talent and ego strained against that limited world. It was bedeviling.

What happened? The answer seemed to lie in the tour the band undertook in 1982, in support of its first (and, as it turned out, only) major-label album, *Unveiled*. The tour began in eastern Canada and worked west toward British Columbia, playing fifteen-thousand-seat hockey arenas. The Brides had always headlined, but following music-industry standard they were booked to open for a more established act—in this case, Chilliwack, whom you might think of as the Canadian version of, say, Bread. At the time, the Brides' manager was a former schoolteacher of Paul Martin's named Gord Nicholl. Nicholl believed in the fake-it-until-you-make-it approach to artist management, and for the Brides' first national tour he secured a gleaming new Highway Coach bus. As it happened, Chilliwack's road crew—the same crew that would be handling lights and sound for the Brides—was driving a crumbling Winnebago and didn't take kindly to the opening act riding in a luxurious Highway Coach. "I was told in so many words by Chilliwack's road manager that if we proceeded in that coach, for the rest of the tour we would look like shit onstage and sound even worse," Gord Nicholl recalled when I called him one afternoon at home in Ontario. "It was a bad spot to be in. I couldn't negotiate it. I went on the bus and told the guys and they reluctantly agreed to give the bus to Chilliwack's crew and instead took the Winnebago. At four o'clock in the morning, I got a call from Wawa, Ontario. I don't know if you've ever been to Ontario, but it's so big that it takes two days to drive through. Well, anyway, the engine on the Winnebago had blown and the band had a tour stop the next day in Thunder Bay."

The bus was a harbinger of things to come. Morale was low even before the tour began; by then, everyone was burned out from being on the road for three years solid. Also, there was displeasure in the band with the way the debut album had turned out. Once, in describing *Unveiled,* Maurice said, "Most of the songs are shit I wrote when I was a fucking kid, like fifteen. There are only about five songs that cut the mustard." I tracked down a copy of *Unveiled* on LP and have spent many hours listening to it and studying the peculiar cover, which shows three attractive women, each sitting under one of those fifties-style conical-shaped hair dryers, dressed in wedding gowns, like blushing brides. I don't find *Unveiled* as wanting as Maurice does. In fact, I like a lot of the songs—especially a number called "Run and Hide," which has some wonderfully slinky guitar playing by Paul Martin, and a melancholy ballad, "Can't Come Back." The first single, a funk-reggae tune called "What You Talkin' Bout?" received radio airplay in Canada. Like a lot of albums from the eighties, the production is crisp and bright, and in the studio Maurice's voice is even more powerful than it is live.

Unveiled is a perfectly fine debut. The problem, I think, is that the material isn't the Stones—that is, for three years the Brides had been performing the greatest rock songs ever put down on tape. How could they have recorded anything to equal "Satisfaction" or "Brown Sugar," especially since the band members were just learning how to write songs and navigate the complexities of the studio? By becoming so popular through playing Stones music, the band set an impossibly high (and false) standard for itself. As a Stones band, they were a sensation; by switching to their own music, they were starting all over. This became frustratingly apparent during the Chilliwack tour. Each night, the Brides played to audiences who had never heard of them and who were naturally tepid in their reaction.

As the tour progressed, a rift developed within the band. Paul Martin and the other members wanted to forge ahead and play the songs from *Unveiled* to establish themselves as original artists, while Maurice argued to include more Stones numbers to win crowds. The disagreement was complicated by the fact that the record company expected the Brides to promote their debut album, which did not mean playing Stones covers on the band's first national tour. With each succeeding concert, relations between Maurice and the rest of the band grew more fraught. Each night, an argument ensued over the set list, sometimes onstage. Slowly, the musicians began to fall back on what they knew best. "I think the band played a forty-minute set, and in that set there were going to be two Stones songs," Dickie Kahl, who was the band's road manager at the time and later the Brides' rhythm guitarist, told me. "That percentage grew over the course of the tour, because when a night didn't go great, there was pressure to resort to something that would get the crowd reaction the band was used to. The thinking was that maybe it would rub off on the original songs."

By the time the tour reached western Canada, the Brides were in the midst of an identity crisis. Were they a Stones tribute? An original rock band? Some murky thing in between? Finally, one night after a show, Maurice said, "That's it, I've had enough," and flew home to Montreal, quitting the tour. Without a singer, the rest of the band had no choice but to cancel the remaining few dates. The Brides had signed a five-album deal with RCA. But by not playing their own songs they had, in effect, breached their own contract, and months later—by which time the remaining members had fired Maurice and hired another singer—they were dropped from the label. Some members eventually reconciled two years later, including Maurice and Paul Martin, and along with new musicians, the Brides soldiered on. But the band never really recovered from the Chilliwack tour, and later attempts to fold their own songs into the tribute shows felt awkward and forced.

Toward the end of my conversation with Gord Nicholl, the band's manager, I asked him why he thought the Brides had such difficulty moving beyond their most formative influence. Gord said: "If you're a writer first and a performer second, you have a greater ease going from cover songs to your own material. But I think the Brides' talent lay more in performing, and it was complicated by the fact that they did it so amazingly, probably better than anyone else." The phone was silent for a moment. "I think the lesson is that it's okay to be a tribute band," Gord said finally, "but don't do it too well. You may never be able to do anything else."

I saw the Brides perform one more time after that night in Fall River, on a Saturday in mid-November. They were booked to play a fan's sixtieth birthday party at an Elks lodge in rural Massachusetts. On the drive up from New York City that day, the mood was understandably downbeat: no one joins a rock and roll band to play a sixtieth birthday party at an Elks lodge.

In late afternoon, Maurice exited I-95 in Rhode Island and we drove through a town of dirty brick buildings and vinyl-sided houses, the sort of charmless place people spend their teenage years vowing to escape as soon as they are grown. Passing a drugstore whose sign read HOWELL SMITH: DRUGGIST, Shane looked at Rodney, the drummer, and said, "Rodney Ledbetter: Drug Addict," and everyone laughed, breathing some levity into the day. After a brief complication with the MapQuest directions, Maurice regained his bearings, crossed the Massachusetts state line, turned off the main highway, and drove up a forested street that ended at a low-slung, nearly windowless concrete building: Elks Lodge 1014.

"Are we before or after the puppet show?" Shane said as we parked in front.

"We are the puppet show," Lee Boice said.

The band went inside to have a look at the place, which was empty at that hour, except for a few old men drinking in a bar in back. Maurice stayed in the van by himself. Later, as the musicians set up their gear, I walked to a nearby convenience store and saw Maurice still sitting alone in the van. He was staring off into the distance blankly and appeared to be bracing himself, storing up emotional reserves in the manner of someone about to go through a draining experience—say, a funeral.

The man celebrating his sixtieth birthday that night was a lively, bespectacled oral surgeon named Joel, who bore a resemblance to the talk-show host Jerry Springer. Later that night, I watched a woman hold Joel's legs like you would hold the handles of a wheelbarrow as he did push-ups in time to the music. In addition to the Brides, a DJ had been hired, and around nine o'clock, after everyone had eaten, Joel took the DJ's microphone and addressed the packed room of his friends. "We've got the Blushing Brides," he said as the band waited in the wings. "They're a great band and we're going to party into the night!"

Without a word of introduction, the band launched into "Little Queenie," then "Let Me Down Slow," a song from the Stones' new album, which the musicians had worked up during the sound check. Just like Uncle Leo's birthday party a few weeks before, the celebrants were weighted down with food and remained seated. "Loosen up. Shake what Mama gave you," Maurice told the crowd when he finally spoke. His tone was joyless and slightly admonishing. "Nobody's here. There's no cops. No parents. Well, some of you are parents, but pretend you're not. Have a good time."

Maurice did not follow his own advice: shortly into the set, he turned and began to dog Rodney Ledbetter about his drumming and became visibly irritated. The other band members looked uneasy and seemed to shrink into themselves so as to not draw Maurice's ire. Then, during one of Lee Boice's long guitar solos, Maurice walked to the back of the room, turned his back on the crowd, and stood an inch from the wall, in the manner of a misbehaving schoolboy ordered to the corner. He just stood there, staring at the wall. It seemed an eternity.

At the intermission, the DJ took over. "A job well done, fellas," the DJ said in an unctuous tone as the Brides retreated to their dressing room. "Meanwhile," the DJ went on, "the dance floor is officially open again. Time to get *funky*. Time to get *loose*. A little 'Brick House' going out to the ladies"—here the DJ cued up the old Commodores hit—"and ladies, remember, if you have any requests, bring them up to the DJ booth. Don't be shy. We do not *bite*."

She's a brick ta da-da-da-da HOUSE . . .

Out in the lobby, I ran into Joe Scammon, the longtime Brides fan I'd met that summer at the Speakeasy on Cape Cod. "I had a helluva time finding this place," Joe said. "It's in the middle of nowhere." We exchanged a knowing look. Joe shook his head sadly and said, "I never thought I'd see the Brides play an Elks lodge."

I felt for Maurice and for the other band members, Shane, Lee, Daniel Hoffenberg, and Rodney Ledbetter. They deserved better. They were good players, and they cared about their craft and had made great sacrifices to pursue the life of a musician. I was thinking about this during the band's second set, which had continued much as the first had, with Maurice angry and the band on edge and a dark cloud hanging over the bandstand, when a strange thing happened. Like a terrible fever that suddenly breaks, Maurice's bad mood lifted—just like that, as if a switch had been thrown. Watching him, there was a physical transformation: his whole body slackened and his face brightened. He began joking with the crowd. He sweetly teased a teenage girl dancing with her boyfriend. He seemed enlivened, joyful, filled with a renewed desire to perform. One of the last things I wrote in my notebook that night was a description of Maurice singing "Tumbling Dice." His head was tilted back defiantly. His left hand was planted firmly on his hip, his right hand clutched the microphone on its stand. His hair was sweaty and matted to his forehead. *"You've got to roll me,"* he was singing, going at it full bore, pouring himself into the song, as Joel and his friends were dancing and having a good time. It brought to mind something else that Gord Nicholl had told me. When the Brides were starting out, Gord said, Maurice used to tell him, "Look at me. You can put me under a streetlamp and I'll dazzle people." And it was true.

11

During the year I followed Sticky Fingers, the band nearly broke up—twice. The first occasion followed a concert the group played in September at a casino in West Virginia, a show tied to the Stones tour, which was passing through nearby. For a working band, casino engagements are prized because the one thing casinos have is money, and so they tend to pay well and without giving the musicians much hassle. Also, casinos are often owned by large conglomerates, and they are in constant need of distractions to entertain gamblers, which means going over well in one can lead to bookings in others. It happened to be the first time Sticky Fingers had played this particular casino—the Mountaineer Racetrack and Gaming Resort in Chester, West Virginia—and Glen was adamant that the band be on time and give a professional performance that would impress the manager. He'd arrived a day early with Lisa and made the trip into a mini-vacation. Dan, Kevin, and George, meanwhile, scrambled to get there on time because the show was on a weekday and Kevin couldn't leave until after work, and then he and Dan had to pick up George in New Jersey and race across three states.

After all that, the casino turned out to be a letdown—"not what you'd call up to Las Vegas standards," is how Dan described it. The stage was elevated fifteen feet above the casino bar, so no one could really see the band. Most people didn't seem to mind, anyway; as Sticky Fingers played, the crowd pumped quarters into the slot machines. Glen became morose. He began to drink. Then people bought him more drinks during the intermission, so he drank more. A lot of state troopers happened to be in the casino that night, and during the second set Glen seemed to delight in provoking them from the stage, saying things like "Fuck the man" and "If you're going to drive home drunk, drive fast," his classic line at frat houses. Shortly after the band started "You Can't Always Get What You Want," Glen disappeared for an uncomfortably long period of time. The musicians continued playing so as not to alert the audience that the band was missing its singer. Then someone looked down at the floor, where Glen was passed out, drunk. When casino employees tried to revive him, Glen took a swing at them. The band had to finish the show without him; the casino staff came out with one of those boards used for spinal-injury victims and carried Glen away.

The incident at the casino deeply unsettled the other band members. On the drive home that night—out his pay, racing to get Kevin back for work the next morning, driving through a hellacious thunderstorm—Dan announced to Kevin and George that he was quitting the band. According to Kevin, who told me the casino story later (I wasn't there), what Dan actually said was, "Unless Glen calls me up and licks my fucking balls, that's it. That's my last job."

Later that week, George quit, too. Kevin didn't commit one way or the other (he relied desperately on the money), but he'd begun to quietly investigate teaming with another Mick Jagger, one who didn't behave so erratically and get the band into troubling situations. There were other complaints: Kevin was growing frustrated over Glen's limited selection of songs—the tribute world equivalent of creative differences—and Dan felt he was paying the band's travel expenses without timely reimbursement. Glen responded to criticism with a my-way-or-the-highway obstinacy. And, too, he said the other members had no idea the labor involved in running a steady working band like Sticky Fingers: cozying up to agents and promoters, hustling up gigs, working out the most cost-effective travel arrangements, which were usually the most convoluted. I sometimes wondered why the musicians didn't quit, why they put up with the exhausting travel schedules and meager financial and creative returns. They all had pressing real-life concerns beyond the band. Dan had received a financial settlement after his on-the-job injury, but the money would eventually run out and he'd likely have to find another job. Kevin had moved back to Queens, believing that his wife and two boys would join him, but his wife didn't want to leave Chicago, and so his marriage was falling apart. George, meanwhile, was working dead-end jobs and spinning his wheels. As for Glen, it was true he lived a low-altitude version of the rock star life, but he was in his forties, with no retirement plan, no stability, no musical legacy of his own. How much longer could he go on pretending to be Mick Jagger? Unlike recording acts, which generate revenue from publishing royalties and album sales, tribute bands earn money only through performing. As long as he fronted Sticky Fingers, Glen could never stop hustling gigs, never quit playing the frat houses and town fairs.

I sensed the reason they remained in the band was because they weren't ready to give up the small rewards being a member of Sticky Fingers provided them: a degree of local renown; the chance to perform to enthusiastic crowds; a taste of what it was like to be a rock star. In the past year, Sticky Fingers had been to Houston, Atlanta, Las Vegas, Los Angeles, and Europe, among other places, and the band was scheduled to fly to San Francisco, where the musicians would be met at the airport by a limousine. Many, many rock bands are formed. Very few of them are ever met at the airport by a limo. Glen had a knack for scoring great gigs. Who knew what lay ahead? There was talk of the band going to China. *China!* The simple fact was that life in Sticky Fingers was more exciting than life outside of it.

A week after the casino show, George was fired from his job painting houses; ironically, his boss said he was missing too much work because of his involvement in the band. With no income, he called Glen and asked to rejoin. And while Glen didn't exactly lick Dan's balls, he did apologize to the band for his behavior at the casino. Soon, "the leading international Rolling Stones tribute show" was back together again.

One day around that time, I called Glen at home in Florida to find out when Sticky Fingers was scheduled to perform again. No one answered the phone, but a machine picked up and a British-accented female voice said, " 'Ello, and thank you for calling

Made in the Shade Productions. We're either on the other line or you've reached us after business hours. Please leave a message and we'll return your call as soon as possible. Thank you." I'd never heard of Made in the Shade Productions, but when I eventually reached Glen, he explained that his new girlfriend, Lisa, was handling the band's bookings now (as well as singing backup) and that they were moving in together. Then he told me that Sticky Fingers would be appearing in Charlotte, North Carolina, on Friday, October 21; the Stones were playing in the city that night and Sticky Fingers was doing a preconcert bash at a local bar.

On that Friday morning, I drove into Manhattan to pick up Kevin Gleeson, who was riding with me. When I pulled up to the corner where we'd agreed to meet, he was standing on the street, already dressed as Keith, as was his custom. It was 4 A.M. The drive to Charlotte would take ten hours, all of it on boring interstate, and we passed the time by listening to country music on the radio and talking about our favorite Stones albums and songs. I favored the classic period between 1968 and 1972, when Mick Taylor was the band's guitarist and before Keith Richards's drug addiction eroded his musical gifts. Kevin favored everything.

For the ride, he brought with him a CD of songs he'd written himself and recorded at a friend's home studio. The songs had a scruffy charm and sounded not unlike Keith Richards's solo work. "This is about a girl who used to come over to my house," he said of one song. "Her boyfriend was the bass player in a famous band and she used to sleep with me. You can't blame a girl that loves getting naked. It was so generous of her."

In North Carolina, we spotted a billboard advertising a barbecue eatery and exited the interstate and went driving down a two-lane road in search of pulled pork. On the way, Kevin said, "You know, we're like Keith and Spanish Tony, having adventures." He was referring to Spanish Tony Sanchez, who for many years was Richards's drug dealer and running buddy. The comment gave me pause. I'd been issued my own tribute band identity, which I have to admit I found a bit touching, although the parallels troubled me: Tony Sanchez wrote a tell-all book about the Stones, *Up and Down with the Rolling Stones,* and when it was published, Richards reportedly slugged him.

Around four o'clock, we arrived in Charlotte and found Dixie's Tavern, the bar where Sticky Fingers was performing. It was in an old redbrick building set alone on an open block downtown. A professional stage had been built in the large parking lot beside the bar, with speaker columns attached to metal rigging and lights suspended from a canopy roof. On a backdrop behind the drums hung a banner that said STICKY FINGERS and, under that, in smaller type, THE GREATEST ROCK 'N' ROLL TRIBUTE BAND IN THE WORLD.

Glen was standing on the lip of the stage. He was holding a beer in one hand and looking out over the scene in the manner of a military general surveying a soon-to-be-conquered land. That day, he wore a black Harley-Davidson T-shirt, blue jeans, sunglasses, and a silver-studded belt. It was a sunny, cloudless afternoon. There was a festive mood in the air because construction had just been completed on the new Charlotte Bobcats Arena and the Stones concert was to christen the building. Charlotte's classic rock station, WRFX "the Fox," was broadcasting live from Dixie's to mark the occasion. Towering over the parking lot was the station's mascot, a thirty-foot-high inflatable orange fox wearing pink sunglasses and holding a guitar. *"This has just been so much fun, nothing but Stones tunes!"* the DJ was saying from his mobile broadcast tent. *"Mr. Bill and the Fox live for you at the official Stones preconcert party here at Dixie's Tavern, about a block and a half south of the new arena. And if you haven't seen the new arena, it's just amazing!"*

In fact, the arena was so close to Dixie's that the Stones could have stood outside and heard their own songs played back to them. I sometimes wondered if the Stones were aware of Sticky Fingers—if they knew another band was shadowing them across the country, singing their songs, entertaining their fans. The two bands were performing less than two blocks away from each other that night—the closest they would come all tour—but the distance between them felt vast and unbridgeable. I briefly entertained the thought of Mick Jagger and Keith Richards sneaking over to Dixie's to watch Sticky Fingers, or, better, jumping onstage to sit in with the band. I imagine Glen has entertained the thought, too. But he has also played enough preconcert parties at places like Dixie's to know it would be unlikely.

In the mobile radio tent, Mr. Bill was interviewing a guy nicknamed Professor Stones who taught a course on the Stones at a local community college. I listened to the interview, then went inside Dixie's and up to Sticky Fingers' dressing room on the second floor. The band members were seated around a wooden table, smoking cigarettes and talking idly. Glen's girlfriend, Lisa, had on black leather pants and a matching leather halter, like a motorcycle mama. On the table in front of her were typed copies of that night's set list with the words BOOKINGS: MS. LISA KENNEDY across the top.

"So the first set starts with 'Honky Tonk'?" Dan asked.

"That's the second set," Glen said. "First set starts with 'Satis-faction.' " Glen turned to George, who had his long hair pulled back into a ponytail. "George, not the ponytail onstage, man."

"I know," George said. "I'm trying to stay cool in the heat."

"I just don't want that Allman Brothers look onstage any-more. We have important shows coming up," Glen said, referring to a Hurricane Katrina charity concert the band was performing the next night at a minor league baseball stadium in San Francisco. The conversation turned to the fact that George had been fired from his house-painting job, and how his boss had cited the band's travel schedule as the reason. "That cocksucker is just jealous," Glen said. "I told George to move down to Florida, where he can sun his nads, ride his bike."

"Well," George said, "now he wants me to come back to work. He plays guitar, so he loves to hear all the road stories and travels and shit."

"He plays the skin flute," Glen said, and cleared his throat loudly. "All right, everybody. Ten minutes to show time!"

Dan fiddled nervously with the buttons on his shirt. "This is always the worst time, right before the show," he said. "They tell you ten minutes; then it's a half hour. At the Ted Turner gig in Atlanta, we had six hours to kill before we went on. I don't know what they thought was going to happen. It was an open bar. This band does not do well with time to kill and an open bar."

A good-sized crowd had gathered outside to drink beer and hear Stones music before seeing the Stones. But everyone oddly stood fifty feet from the stage, leaving a gulf between the band and the audience—the sort of subtly divisive factor that kills a concert before it begins. "Are you ready for the breakfast show?"

Glen yelled when the band took the stage, but the crowd shuffled lazily and remained at a remove, as if saving their energy for the main event later that night.

When Sticky Fingers returned to the stage after an hour break, the mood had changed and a sudden drama overtook the night. Spotlights crisscrossed the darkened sky, coming from the direction of the new arena; overhead, a helicopter circled, and for a brief moment it felt like all the clamor was meant for Sticky Fingers, not the Stones. The crowd at Dixie's, helped along by many beers, had loosened up (so had Glen, who was drinking Southern Comfort from a plastic cup), and the music was made urgent by the insistent thwacking of the helicopter's blades. The guitars seemed louder somehow. Dan's drumming was more powerful. The band blistered through rockers like "Brown Sugar" and "Start Me Up." When they played "You Can't Always Get What You Want," Professor Stones and his date slow-danced in the middle of the parking lot. During the first set, a man from the audience had randomly walked onstage and sung backup vocals on several songs with Lisa. No one had invited him, but no one told him to leave, either. Now he returned and stayed for the rest of the show, singing exuberantly—and off-key—with an exaggerated grin on his face. The band finished with the most ragged version of "Can't You Hear Me Knocking" I have ever heard. It sounded like a combustion engine in the throes of complete mechanical failure. Mr. Bill was moved to come out from behind his DJ booth and jam a few bars of air guitar. Two rock chicks shimmied in front of the stage. When I turned to look at the crowd's reaction, I saw that the parking lot behind me was empty; everyone else had left for the Stones concert.

Up in the band's dressing room after the show, Glen said, "These people weren't into us. I can't blame them. They got the real deal a hundred yards away."

"No way, man," George said. He lit up a cigarette, took a drag, exhaled. "We gave them a fucking great show."

"Yeah, yeah, yeah," Glen said dismissively. "We're only competing with the greatest rock and roll band in the world, right? I remember a gig like this near the Fleet Center in Boston four years ago, and those are the toughest critics you'll ever play in front of. They don't want to hear *shit but the Stones.* They're about to see the Stones and they're thinking, You're not the Stones. You still catch them digging it, but they're trying not to. Now, we're going out to San Francisco in the morning, and those people haven't had their Stones fix yet. They'll go nuts."

"All I know is, not only did we do our job; we did an outstanding example of our job," Dan said.

Glen changed out of his stage clothes. "Did you see that tall blonde standing in front of the stage?" he said. *"Oh my God."*

"Yeah, where did she go?" George said. "She was with some Dilbert. She didn't want to be hanging with that dude. She wanted to hang with *us.* It was so obvious."

Just then, Lisa walked into the dressing room. "Lisa, you were great tonight," Glen said sweetly, and then, referring to the guy who'd crashed onstage, added, "but that dude ruined the vocals."

"He was *killing* her," Dan said. "Who was that guy? All of a sudden, I look over and he's singing with Lisa. I mean, I thought he was from the Stones' road crew or something." He shook his head. "It's just wrong allowing people to come up onstage like that."

Everyone walked back outside. The spotlights were still swirling across the sky and a few people who didn't have concert tickets were hanging out in the parking lot, drinking beer in the warm night. The band members had an early flight the next morning, so after loading the gear, they drove back to their motel, near the airport. I wasn't going to San Francisco, so I walked over to the arena to see if I could score a ticket to the Stones concert. A handful of people were milling by the front entrance, all semi-desperately searching for tickets. One of them was the man who had jumped onstage with Sticky Fingers. He was tall and twitchy and he introduced himself as Chris, then said, "But everyone calls me Sweet Dick Willy. You ask anybody in Charlotte, they know Sweet Dick." Sweet Dick was with a hippie girl, and he said, "I'm trying to get her a ticket. She ain't never seen the Stones." He looked at the girl tenderly. "I'll get you in, baby, don't worry. By the third song, you'll be sitting in that stadium."

After a moment, everyone standing outside heard the opening riff of "Start Me Up" and a roar from inside the arena; the concert had started. I canvassed the blocks around the stadium in my own semi-desperate search for a ticket, but the scalpers were tapped. When I returned to the stadium entrance, Sweet Dick was counting out bills into a man's hand. Finished, he handed a ticket to the hippie girl and she walked into the arena and paused in the doorway, looking back at Sweet Dick, who stood out on the sidewalk. "Remember who loves you, baby," he yelled to her. "Sweet Dick."

I had felt the momentum of the night carrying me toward

the Stones concert and I became slightly morose at the idea that I would have to listen from the street. But then, miraculously, two girls who had seats in different parts of the arena decided they'd rather not see the concert at all if they couldn't sit together, and after winning a heated bidding war with a scalper, I had a ticket. When I found my seat, I was overjoyed to discover I finally had a seat within spitting distance of the stage.

A week and a half after that show in Charlotte, Dan quit the band again as a result of another misadventure, this time at a Waffle House in Charleston, South Carolina. The band had been enjoying a postgig breakfast, when Glen, fairly soused, remarked loudly, "Rosa Parks didn't do nothing but sit her black ass down," a line from the movie *Barbershop*. Coming, as it did, a few days after Parks's death, and in a restaurant where most of the patrons were black, it was, at the very least, ill-timed. The restaurant went silent in the way Wild West saloons do in movies just before a fight breaks out. Two large black men who had been sitting nearby got up and walked out. The musicians were left to finish their meal wondering if they would be pummeled in the parking lot. "The last thing I'm going to do is play in a band where I'm putting my life in danger," Dan told me later.

It seemed only a matter of time before something very bad happened to the band on the road, although a feeling of looming catastrophe was not unfamiliar. Kenny Aaronson once told me, dramatically, "Every time I went on the road with Sticky Fingers, I feared for my life." Kenny spent the seventies touring as a bassist with Foghat and Rick Derringer and had played on the same bill as Led Zeppelin, so I found it hard to believe Glen Carroll was the most excessive rock and roll personality he'd ever encountered. But he explained, "In a professional situation, you've got a crew, you've got minders. There's always someone there to put you to bed or watch over you or keep you from being arrested. They can head off the real bad stuff most of the time. But when you're out on the road with a low-end band . . ."

A few days after the Charleston episode, Dan sent Glen and the other band members an E-mail message, laying out his issues with the band and his conditions for rejoining. The E-mail said:

1. PAY: when the gig is over, we should all get paid, case closed. All the crap revolving around checks, checks versus cash, etc, just makes us all later to leave, and engenders bad vibes. When we finish our work, <u>we all expect to get paid</u>, not to have to ask, wheedle or cajole to get our pay. This is a business, and should be run like one where this is concerned.

2. LODGING: I don't know when the musicians staying over became a personal expense, but I for one am not going to continue paying for a room for myself only. Two rooms is now a necessity, and in my view, is part of the cost of running the band. Whatever Jazzkat does is not my personal problem or concern, and having 5 of us stay in one room is out of the question.

3. PERSONAL DEMEANOR: I love to rock, and I love to party, and there's a place for both. Insulting people is not part of that, and can get us all in very serious trouble, hurt, or worse. I will not encourage, defend or explain anyone's bad behavior, whether in a Waffle House, a hotel, or at the venue. And if that's not acceptable, then an-

other drummer needs to be found. We each have a responsibility to comport ourselves professionally.

4. SHOW ITSELF: I personally have no strong feelings about what happens at any particular show, except that we each do our job, and I hold up my end, and get paid for my work. I think you all know that I go above the call to try to make things as smooth and professional as possible, and after that, it's all good. But I do not believe Mick ever plays drums, the Stones would play a Black Crowes tune at soundcheck, or that just because we shuffle the order of the songs, we are changing the show. It's always the same songs and, frankly, 8 Keith songs is crazy. It's not my place to dictate band policy, I am just sharing my own feelings about our *Tribute Band* show. And for chrissakes, let's all <u>learn the songs</u>, please? "Can't You Hear Me . . ." is a disaster, "T&A" is just always terrible, and the added middle section of "Satisfaction" just really brings me down, to name a few. One more thing: purposely not playing songs that the audience ALWAYS requests, and which go over very big (like "Queenie," "Imagination," and "Beast of Burden") is just not good business, whether you like the song or not.

————

The next day, Glen fired off a long E-mail reply, addressing each point, which said, in part:

[PAY:] Most all professional businesses withhold an employee's paycheck two weeks before dispersing them so taxes and other factors can be dealt with. With the exception of prostitutes and crack dealers, how many workers get cash stuffed into their hand at the end of a workday? When I receive a check it isn't the same thing as "being paid." All I have is a piece of paper that hopefully will clear in five business days if it doesn't bounce. . . . If you have to have a check or cash for every gig we play the night of the gig, **PLEASE DON'T WORK FOR ME!**

[LODGING:] I always have beds for at least four people and I'm always willing to sleep on a rollaway or on the floor. I have no problem with that. When I started this band, we used to sleep in our vans with sleeping bags. . . . Just knowing there's at least one safe dry room is good enough for me. I'm not the Rolling Stones and I don't have their budget. . . . Anyone that doesn't want to share a room or pay for it themselves, **PLEASE DON'T WORK FOR ME!**

[PERSONAL DEMEANOR:] People that live in glasshouses, **PLEASE DON'T WORK FOR ME!**

[SHOW ITSELF:] The Stones aren't playing Beast of Burdon [*sic*] so who says we have to? Imagination and Queenie aren't even songs by the Rolling Stones to begin with, and are we supposed to drop Honky Tonk Women or Jumping Jack so we can play them? . . . If you can't play the songs I need played, **PLEASE DON'T WORK FOR ME!** . . . My phone is still going to ring no matter how great or bad a show goes. That I have learned after twenty-five years. It's never been because I have had any members contribute something. It is because there is demand for me. Can you say that about yourself? Can you find another working band that wants you today that will pay you every night after your gig, get you your own bed, play the songs you want to play even if they don't want to and never do anything you find insulting? Good luck. If you can find one, **PLEASE DON'T WORK FOR ME!**

Dan heeded the bold print. He quit Sticky Fingers and concentrated on his own tribute bands—to Blondie, to R.E.M, and to the Ramones. I went one night to see his R.E.M. tribute, the Buck Stipes Here, at a bar above a strip club near Wall Street. About ten people showed up and the band sounded weirdly out of sync, although I couldn't put my finger on why; later, Dan told me the guitar player was deaf in both ears.

Two months passed. Glen hired various fill-in drummers to replace Dan, and Sticky Fingers continued as usual. Over Thanksgiving weekend, the band performed at the home of a St. Louis man who had turned his basement into a replica of a 1950s soda shop. On New Year's Eve, they played a club in St. John, New Brunswick, Canada, and were searched at the border on their way back into the United States (a result, perhaps, of Kevin not taking off his Keith costume?). Jazzkat took over Dan's duties as road manager and bought a minivan to haul the band, which, given the tenuous nature of Sticky Fingers membership, seemed a questionable purchase. I saw the band perform at a pool hall in a strip mall near Hartford around this time, and it was strange not to see Dan there. Sticky Fingers felt incomplete somehow, although no one else seemed fazed by his absence. "Dan tried to take over the empire," Jazzkat told me. "Glen is the boss. Glen signs the checks. I said, 'Dan, I'm not looking for regime change.'"

Then, one day in January, I got a call from Kevin, who said the band had another engagement at Washington and Lee University in Virginia that weekend and Dan would be driving; he and Glen had evidently patched up their differences.

"The issues haven't changed," Dan told me on the drive to Virginia. "But if I only have to see him for two hours, it won't be that bad." Dan said he'd rejoined the band with one caveat: after each show, he planned on packing up his drums and driving straight home. "If I leave right after the gig, Glen and I will get along like peas and carrots," Dan said.

"It's really about the Stones' music," Kevin said.

"That's right," Dan said. He seemed to consider the point. "Even the Stones don't like each other half the time."

During the trip, when Kevin or George mentioned something that involved one of the shows Dan had missed, he listened with jealous interest. And when Kevin remarked that he was trying to get the band an engagement in Chicago, based on his contacts there, Dan said sarcastically, "What contacts do *you* have in Chicago? What gigs have *you* ever gotten the band?"

Kevin seemed wounded. "I know people," he said. "I gave Lisa a list of names."

"Yeah, that's right," Dan said, "you gave Lisa a list. One more thing you didn't take personal responsibility for."

"Why are you being so nasty?" Kevin said.

"Because I'm still mad at you for not backing me up two months ago and I'm working it out," Dan said.

At one point, we pulled into a rest stop and everyone ordered hamburgers from McDonald's. Back on the highway, Kevin said, "I don't eat much. A lot of times, I don't have any money left after I send my paycheck to my wife in Chicago. Sometimes I won't eat for three or four days, like I'm fasting. It helps me clear my thoughts and go inward. I find out where I am and what I'm about."

There was a long silence in the car. Then George said, "Sometimes I won't shit for three or four days. It helps me find out where I am and what I'm about. Then I realize I'm full of shit."

Everyone laughed, especially Dan. He seemed deeply pleased to be back with the band. "See, that's why I do this," he said. "I know I'm going to hear you guys say things I won't hear anywhere else."

The show that night was at Sigma Alpha Epsilon, the same fraternity house that the band had played the previous spring. When we pulled into the driveway, two college guys were standing on the street outside, naked but for boxer shorts, shivering in the cold. Pledge night.

Dan set up his drums in the frat house basement, and when Glen arrived with Lisa, he hugged her dramatically, as if reuniting with a long-lost friend. Then he and Glen began to talk uneasily about a new drum kit Dan had recently bought that was similar to the one Charlie Watts used.

"It's a nice kit," Glen said, not making eye contact with Dan.

"It's maple," Dan said proudly, "and the cymbals have rivets so they'll sizzle, just like Charlie's." In that same vein, he said, he was searching eBay for a Rogers "Swiv-o-Matic" hi-hat stand.

"Yep," Glen said, "it's a nice kit."

Just before the band went on, Glen turned to me and said, "You watch this first set. It's taken me twenty years to put something like this together." He took the stage like a caged animal that had been released, singing in a loud, crisp voice, snapping into Jagger poses. Midway through the first set, he looked out at the fraternity kids, who were dancing with abandon, and said affectionately into the microphone, *"You rock and roll motherfuckers."*

During the set break, the band crowded into their dressing area, a cramped little basement laundry room. A few of the older frat brothers took over the stage to hold a striptease contest featuring the pledges. Some minutes later, one of the pledges, a fat kid, came into the laundry room, drunk and shirtless. "I love the Stones," he slurred. "I even got a dog named Jagger." He turned and stared at Glen hazily. "You're a great Mick, man."

Glen was leaning against the wall, holding a bottle of Southern Comfort. "That's all I ever wanted to be was a great Mick," he said, managing to sound both disingenuous and sincere, then took a long pull from the bottle.

By the start of the second set, Glen was happily drunk. He began to make exaggerated faces as he sang, pushing his lips out like a fish, his eyes ping-ponging around in their sockets. The music became slack, like a cord that had been stretched out of shape. When the band did "Can't You Hear Me Knocking," Glen decided he wanted to play the drums; he beat on the cymbals enthusiastically, then began playfully hitting Dan with the drumsticks, beating time on his shoulders and belly. He was tanked.

When the show ended, Glen walked to his van, which was parked in the driveway, and Dan and Kevin began packing up their instruments. George and I were standing in a stairwell that led to the upstairs. It was after midnight and the party was clearing out. The basement smelled like stale beer. A couple was sitting on the stairwell, kissing. The scene seemed to make George melancholy. "What happened to me?" he said suddenly. "I was supposed to be a rock star."

George stood in the hallway and considered the course his life had taken to lead him to this night. Dan walked by carrying a drum case. Kevin was onstage, carefully packing up his guitars. All in all it had been a pleasant night. Suddenly Lisa burst into the room, screaming, *"Somebody help me! There's a fight outside. You've got to stop it."*

"Who's fighting?" Dan asked.

"Glen!" Lisa said, sounding panicked.

We all ran outside into the bitter cold. On the front lawn, near a stand of trees, Glen was stalking after two fraternity brothers who looked terrified. As he moved toward them, fists clenched, his face had a calm but deranged expression, like a predator in a slasher movie. In the middle of the lawn, inexplicably, sat Glen's Dodge Grand Caravan, with tire tracks tracing a sort of figure eight in the mud around it. One of the frat brothers, backpedaling furiously, was yelling, *"Get this guy away from me. He's a maniac!"* Cornered, the frat brother pressed a cell phone to his ear and yelled, "I'm calling the *cops*!"

Glen continued his forward pursuit undaunted. As he neared the frat brother with the cell phone, the other one circled behind and booted Glen in the ass. Lisa was nearly in tears. All of this transpired in seconds but seemed to unfold in slow motion. Finally, Dan ran over and yelled, "Break it up, break it up," and held Glen back while the frat brothers fled to higher ground. Glen, restrained, pointed to the frat brothers and began to scream, "HE KICKED MY VAN! HE KICKED MY VAN!"

Within seconds, the dark street lit up with flashing lights, and three police cars pulled up to the frat house. Several cops jumped out and huffed up the hill. As soon as the police arrived, one of the frat brothers disappeared and the other, the one holding the cell phone, stood on the crest of the lawn, pointing at Glen. The officer in charge walked over to Glen, while another cop interrogated the frat brother. The story, as it emerged, was that Glen's van had been parked in the driveway and he had decided to exit via the frat house lawn. When the frat brothers noticed someone ripping up their front yard, they swung into action, drop-kicking the back of the van. Not that Glen's telling of events was in any way rational—he was waving his arms and yelling at the cops, spittle flying from his mouth. He finished with a verbal crescendo, something to the effect of *"I fought for my country and had men die in my arms and no college boy is going to destroy my property!"* That was when the head officer handcuffed him.

The remaining frat brother, meanwhile, displayed the orderly charm of a Boy Scout. "May I please tell my side of the story, Officer?" he asked politely. If Glen had followed suit, he probably would have driven away with a dent in his van and a hollow promise from the fraternity to repair the damage. Instead, he continued to scream and carry on. He railed at the officers for cuffing him but not the frat brother. He demanded the handcuffs be removed, then tried to squirm loose when the demand went unheeded. Oddly, he began to state emphatically that he was an officer of the law himself and to yell, *"Lisa, get my badge!"* Finally, the officer in charge had had enough. "You're under arrest," he said, and motioned to his men. Two officers lifted Glen off his feet and carried him across the lawn in the way a parent might remove a misbehaving child from a restaurant. Then they shoved him into the backseat of a police cruiser and drove off.

Later, on the ride home, after Glen was taken to the county lockup (he spent the night in jail), and Kevin carefully drove the van off the frat house lawn, and Lisa collected herself and went to see about bailing Glen out, Kevin said, with admiration in his voice, "I'll say one thing about Glen. He don't back down. I mean, he's balls-out rock and roll."

"Well," Dan said, "that's it for me. I don't need this bullshit. Going to jail at a frat house? That's just retarded. This is my last gig. I'm through." There was a long silence. "Who am I kidding?" Dan said, finally. "I'll probably be on the next one. I can't help it. I love it. I love playing to an appreciative crowd."

"I love it, too," George said. "I know this isn't a real band. But it's fun—it feels great to get out there and play."

12

When I first met Glen Carroll, in 2001, and he was living in that big house in Massachusetts, I ended the afternoon by asking him how long he planned to perform in a tribute band. What I meant was, how long did he plan to impersonate Mick Jagger? It seemed like a good summing-up question, and I expected him to say something like "I've had some good times but I can't see this going on much longer" or "I think I've got a few good years left before I hang it up." Instead he was defiant. "I'm going to do this for another twenty years," he said as we stood on the porch. "Every summer you'll see an ad in the *Village Voice*: 'Sticky Fingers, the greatest rock and roll tribute band in the world, seeks musicians. If you have the chops, if you have the looks, we'd like to hear from you.'" Glen's answer surprised me then, and does even more so now, having spent a year in the tribute world. Although I often wished I were onstage with the musicians, and as much as I looked forward to road trips with Sticky Fingers and the Blushing Brides, playing in a tribute band seemed like being in an easy and joyful, but unserious, relationship: at some point, it had to end. Or did it? Glen had been singing in Sticky Fingers for twelve years by the time I met him; five more years had since passed. In that time he had played music for more people, on more stages, than most musicians ever will, and his life was certainly more exciting than it would have been had he never formed Sticky Fingers and instead went back to work at the airplane parts company. Glen seemed to be aware of these truths, and to be sustained by them, in the face of the disappointment and indifference he faced as a tribute musician. On another occasion, as he was packing to drive several hundred miles to play a frat house, I remarked on how it was a long haul for one show. Without missing a beat, Glen said, "It's better than eight hours in an office or on a factory floor." I had to agree.

A week after Glen was arrested, I flew to Florida to visit him at his home there, and to ride with him and Lisa to a Sticky Fingers concert at Auburn University, in Alabama—the last show I spent traveling with the band, as it turned out. During the flight, I tried to picture Glen's house. I envisioned a modest home in a quiet suburban neighborhood, and pictured Glen doing typical suburban things: mowing the lawn, taking out the trash, having a summer cookout—only dressed as Mick Jagger.

At the airport in Orlando, I was met by a driver and after giving him directions we headed south toward Winter Haven, passing signs for SeaWorld and Walt Disney World along the way.

After a few miles, the scenery yielded to orange groves, miles and miles of them, broken up by an occasional shopping plaza or a freshly planted housing development. The landscape of central Florida was mostly flat and more sleepy and rural than the glitzy Florida of popular imagination. On a secondary road not far from Winter Haven, the driver became lost. We pulled into a trailer park and asked directions from a middle-aged couple who were practicing their putting stroke on a slice of green carpet laid out in front of a trailer home. I gave the man the name of Glen's street, and he said, "It sounds like a development." He asked if I knew the name. I didn't, but I remembered that Glen said his house fronted a lake. Then I realized that wasn't any help; there was a lake in every direction, and houses ringing each one, as if great effort had been made on the part of central Florida real estate developers to ensure that all the houses had waterfront views.

Glen's house, when we did find it, was among a cluster of modest one-story dwellings half-hidden behind an orange grove. The house was a white one-story like the others, with green shutters and a manicured hedgerow running along the front. I recognized it as belonging to Glen because I saw his van parked in the driveway; a dent was visible from where the fraternity brother had kicked it the week before. When I knocked on the door, Glen answered wearing a white dress shirt and tie and explained that he'd just returned from the funeral of a relative, an uncle or a cousin—I can't remember which. Lisa was behind him, and before I could set my travel bag down, she said, "Do you want a cocktail?"

The home's decor was curious. On the wall in the front room was a large needlepoint scene of cherubic maidens by a brook, with a castle in the distance. Another picture, a framed print, depicted three young girls skipping down a dirt road with a dog. The couches and chairs were upholstered in a floral pattern, and in one corner stood the kind of curio case used to hold, say, Hummel figurines. In short, it appeared as if an elderly woman had moved out and left behind her furnishings, which more or less turned out to be the case. Glen said his parents had lived in the home until recently, when they'd bought another house a few doors down and given him this one. He had big plans for it. "We're really going to fix this place up," he said as he gave me a tour. "Get a big-screen TV for the living room, a kickin' sound system." Already, he'd begun to hang Sticky Fingers memorabilia on the walls: a poster promoting the shows at the Hard Rock Café in Bali; a photo of himself and a former band mate named English Dan dressed in loose-fitting *Miami Vice*–style outfits, sipping cocktails in the backseat of a car. "This will be a good place for entertaining," Glen said, pointing to a screened-in sunporch with a Jacuzzi and grill. In the backyard was a hammock tied to a tree, a little patch of sand beach, a wooden boat dock, and, beyond that, the lake, Lake Buckeye.

As it happened, Lisa's father, Colin, was visiting that weekend. I'd met him two months earlier, when Sticky Fingers had played the pool hall in Hartford and Colin had come down from Boston, where he lives with his sons. He was an aged and robustly built Englishman with a beard, and he seemed to regard Glen's involvement with his daughter with some suspicion. In Connecticut, Lisa had asked him what he thought of the band's music, to which he'd replied, "Rubbish." Now he was sitting in the living room, drinking a screwdriver and watching a soccer match on the telly at deafening volume.

"Do you want your drink refreshed?" Glen asked, overly solicitous.

Colin nodded.

"How was the first one?" Glen asked.

"Too much water," Colin said, chuckling. "Too much orange juice, too."

Just then, the phone rang. Lisa answered it and began talking to someone who, it became clear, was interested in booking Sticky Fingers. "What's your budget, dah'ling?" she asked, playing up her accent. She jotted down the info, told the caller she would send them a promo kit, hung up, then filled Glen in on the particulars. A man was interested in hiring Sticky Fingers to play a yearly biker rally near Buffalo, which was taking place on June 2—the same day a promoter in California wanted the band to perform at a dog parade in Santa Barbara. "He says the bike rally is a cool time," Lisa told Glen.

"You and I could fly up and the rest of the boys could drive," Glen said. "Throw 'em a few bills for expenses, no worries about booking flights for everyone. What's his budget?"

"Five thousand," Lisa said.

Glen seemed to consider the options. "So it's a biker rally or a dog parade," he said without irony. He mulled the choice over. "I think the bikers are more of a Stones crowd," he said finally.

Glen didn't speak much of the incident at Washington and Lee during my visit, except to say that he'd been wronged by the fraternity brothers and hauled off to jail for no good reason and that a lawyer friend of his was looking into it. He spoke about the events as if he had forgotten that I had been a witness. In the evening, we all sat in the living room and watched a Kevin Bacon movie and Lisa made popcorn. Then Glen cooked some chicken on the grill and read jokes from a novelty desk calendar that reprinted President Bush's malapropisms (ex.: "I don't care about the polls. I don't. I'm going to do what I think what's wrong"). The wholesomeness of the evening was mildly shocking, especially after what had happened at the frat house the week before. Glen seemed so rootless—forever on the road with Sticky Fingers, living with one woman on Cape Cod, then another in New Jersey, now a third in Florida—that I expected his domestic life to be tempestuous. But he and Lisa appeared the picture of middle-American suburban averageness. Yet there was a surreal quality, too, as if they were living a version of American life as depicted in a John Waters film. The last thing I saw before going to bed was Glen standing in a pantry off the kitchen. He was ironing his Mick Jagger costume, carefully steaming the wrinkles out of the black pants and pink blouse, folding them neatly over a hanger.

In the morning, Lisa packed a cooler with sandwiches and Glen loaded up the van for the trip to Auburn. He drove down the street, to his parents' home. Glen senior was in the yard. He and Glen walked to a citrus tree behind the house and picked tangerines for the other band members, who'd set out from New York at seven o'clock the night before and, after driving through the night, were somewhere in Georgia. Glen bagged the tangerines, and he and his father stood around uncomfortably for a minute, as though Glen were a teenager and his father was seeing him off on a big trip. Then Glen hopped in the driver's seat and started up the van.

A mile from his house, Glen pulled off the road to look at a bus for sale, parked in a driveway. The bus was an Eagle, cranberry-and-silver two-tone. Glen got out and looked it over. When he got back in the van, he turned to Lisa and said excitedly, "I've gotta have that baby! We'll fix it up, put some sleeping bunks in there, use it for Sticky Fingers gigs." He sighed. "All my life I've had toy fever."

On the highway, headed to a show, Glen was in his element. He toked on marijuana roaches and cued up a CD mix he'd made for the ride. On hearing Joe Cocker's version of the Randy New-man song "You Can Leave Your Hat On," Glen said, "This is the greatest song about a hooker." He took a toke off the roach. "I saw Joe Cocker in the Charleston Civic Center in 1976. I was sixteen and had a fake ID. Joe Cocker drank a whole pitcher of beer in one gulp. Sing it, brother." We crossed the Georgia state line in the early afternoon. For some reason, perhaps the mari-juana, Glen was more reflective than usual. He began to talk about his solo album—the one he had been working on back when we first met, nearly five years earlier. He said a big-time Hollywood record producer had recently shown interest in his demo CD and that the association could lead to his songs getting played on the radio. "This guy has produced Grammy-winning albums," Glen said reverently. "And he wants to work with *me*? Talk about validation." He slipped his demo into the van's CD player. A song called "I Miss the Good Times" came on. It had a great, foot-tapping beat, with a sinewy guitar line, swelling horns, a saxophone solo, and a catchy sing-along chorus that went:

> *I miss the good times I had with you (I miss the good times)*
> *And when I'm feeling lonely, I think of them and I think of you*
> *I miss the good times I had with you (I miss the good times)*
> *And when you're feeling lonely, do you think about them, too?*

It was a great song! Reminiscent of the Stones but not overly so. It was also clear from the lyrics that it was about Julia, the woman Glen had lived with in Massachusetts, which made listening to it in Lisa's presence a bit awkward. But Glen kicked his feet up on the dash, sparked up another joint, cranked the volume, leaned back in his seat, and soaked in the sound of his own music pouring out of the stereo speakers. When the song ended, he said he couldn't wait until the producer finished mixing it and "I Miss the Good Times" was ready to send to record companies and radio stations. I asked him why he wasn't performing the song already, why he was holding off on pursuing his own music until he could work with a famous producer, which might take months or even years to materialize. I thought the demo version sounded great. Lisa agreed. "No, no," Glen said dismissively. "A professional would hear this and know it was incomplete. It's like if you cook something and have a chef taste it. The chef can tell all the things it needs. This guy in L.A. is going to make it sound like a *record*." He was quiet for a moment, then said, "I want my songs to be perfect when people hear them, because you only get one chance to make a first impression."

In Auburn, Lisa drove to a Days Inn downtown where Dan and Kevin had earlier booked a room. (George was staying with Jazz-kat in a hotel nearby.) Glen and Lisa went to the hotel office to get another room. When I knocked on the door to the room where Dan and Kevin were staying, Dan answered with shaving cream on his face. Kevin was asleep in bed. They had driven sixteen hours nonstop from New York; later that night, after the show, Dan and Kevin would load up their equipment at 3:00 A.M.

and the three of us would drive sixteen hours back. After a few minutes, Kevin awoke and went to the mirror and began to get Keithed up. "My kids never liked this very much," he said, dabbing his face with Avon scrub and putting on his jewelry and stage shirt, a teal blue one. "Oh, they like the Stones all right. I just don't think they like *daddy being a Stone*." He laughed his bronchial laugh. Dan sat on the bed and watched a TV show about the porn star Jenna Jameson. Soon it was time to leave for the concert at the Auburn chapter of the Sigma Nu fraternity.

The fraternity house was a massive brick structure on the edge of campus. Behind the house was a parking lot and, at the far end of the lot, a pitch-roofed shed where the fraternity held its parties. When we pulled in, some frat brothers were shuffling across the parking lot toward the shed, lugging a cast-iron smoker—to roast a pig, as it turned out. Dan and Kevin began to set up their equipment inside the shed. The interior had the brute functionality of an auto body shop. The wall, the stage, the doors—everything—had been painted black, except the floor, which was cement. Outside on the patio, the frat brothers set up the smoker, then gathered around a picnic table covered with a garbage bag. Atop the bag lay a newly slaughtered pig. Its skin was nearly transparent and wrinkled, like wet paper. I asked one of the frat brothers if the pig roast marked a special occasion. "No," he said, "we do it every year. Basically, it's an excuse for us to get coked up and stay up all night and drink."

Glen and Lisa arrived shortly thereafter, followed by George and Jazzkat. We all stood on the patio and watched as the frat brothers prepared the pig, coating it with olive oil and seasoning, then hoisting it into the smoker. For the rest of the night, the breeze carried the acrid smell of burning flesh.

The band members went into the shed to do a sound check. When they were finished, Glen came over to me and said suddenly, "This is going to be a good year. I'm going to cut down on my drinking. I've got to learn not to drink a bottle of whiskey when I perform. I get buzzed, and once I get buzzed, I can't tell how drunk I'm getting. But it's hard. My job is to throw a party. It's what I do." He watched the college kids beginning to fill the shed—guys in khakis and southern girls in slinky dresses and heels. "I don't know how many shows I have left," Glen said. "I want to make them great, be able to focus on the moment."

That night, the band didn't seem to want to quit playing. Not to put too fine a point on it, but there was a joy in the music, a spirit clearly audible in the notes, as if everything fractious that had taken place among the musicians over the past few months had been forgotten when they walked onstage. "Jumpin' Jack Flash," "Start Me Up," "Brown Sugar," "Honky Tonk Women," "You Can't Always Get What You Want," "Little T & A." The sound from the amplifiers bounced around the big shed like a pinball. "Paint It, Black," "Sympathy for the Devil," "Thru and Thru," "Satisfaction."

When the party moved out to the parking lot or to points elsewhere, Sticky Fingers kept on playing anyway. "Dead Flowers," "Miss You," "Bitch," "Wild Horses." George stepped to the microphone and said, "What time is it? Two o'clock in the morning? We eat two o'clock in the morning for breakfast!"

And the remaining drunken frat brothers chanted, "ONE MORE SONG! ONE MORE SONG! ONE MORE SONG!"

I was continually amazed by the dedication the tribute musicians showed toward music and the lengths to which they went in order to be able to perform. There would never be a million-dollar recording contract for any of the musicians I'd spent time with. There would never be a gated estate, a fashion model wife, a world tour, a collection of vintage cars and guitars, or any of the clichés that are supposed to come with the rock stardom they had sought. For all of their effort, their renown did not extend beyond a small circle of people, and, in all likelihood, never would. The Rolling Stones, who moved within a cocooned world of privilege and luxury, would soon be off to South America, the Far East, and Europe. The members of Sticky Fingers and the Blushing Brides, meanwhile, faced near poverty, small crowds, exhausting cross-country drives, and indifference from their peers and the world at large, in exchange for a few dollars and the chance to be onstage for a few hours. It is not without its sublime rewards.

I thought back to the last time I'd seen the Brides perform, at the birthday party in Massachusetts, and the transformation I'd witnessed in Maurice—the way during the course of the show he'd gone from being miserable to appearing almost ecstatically happy. For a while, I thought I was alone in noticing what had happened that night, or perhaps was reading too closely into the moment, or looking for something that was not there. But many weeks later, I mentioned it to Shane, who had noticed Maurice's shifting mood, too. "He finally gave up," Shane said. "He stopped fighting everyone." That is one way to characterize what happened. Another way is to say that even onstage at an Elks lodge in the middle of nowhere, you could receive the joy of playing music.

ACKNOWLEDGMENTS

I am grateful to Andrew Essex, Karen Gordon, John Burkhimer, Brian Raftery, Matthew Mayers, Larry Weissman, Annabel Bentley, Connie Rosenblum, Katie Halleron, Mickey Rapkin, Harold and Margaret Bissman, and to Michael Schmelling, whose shared enthusiasm for the subject and good company made the early reporting a joy. Many thanks to Chris Adams and Vicki Vila, who read drafts of the manuscript and offered valuable advice, and to Kathleen Flynn, who polished the final version. I am especially indebted to Gerry Howard for his editorial guidance and good-natured encouragement during the writing process.

Most of all, I would like to thank my parents, Paul and Sandra Kurutz, for a lifetime of love and support.